A GUIDE TO YOUR SUPREME
POWER

CECIL SUWAL &
MARK BRENER

CBN Media
New York, London

CBN Media.
© 2012. Cecil Suwal and Mark Brener. All rights reserved.

No part of this publication may be reproduced or transmitted in any form or by any means, mechanical or electronic, including photocopying and recording, or by any information storage and retrieval system, without permission in writing from author or publisher (except by a reviewer, who may quote brief passages and/or show brief video clips in a review).

Disclaimer: The Publisher and the Authors make no representations or warranties with respect to the accuracy or completeness of the contents of this work and specifically disclaim all warranties, including without limitation warranties of fitness for a particular purpose. No warranty may be created or extended by sales or promotional materials. The advice and strategies contained herein may not be suitable for every situation. This work is sold with the understanding that the Publisher is not engaged in rendering legal, accounting, or other professional services. If professional assistance is required, the services of a competent professional person should be sought. Neither the Publisher nor the Author shall be liable for damages arising herefrom. The fact that a person, organization or website is referred to in this work or related promotional materials as a citation and/or a potential source of further information does not mean that the Authors or the Publisher endorses the information the organization or website may provide or recommendations it may make. No medical claims are implied about any methods, exercises, or techniques suggested in this book, even if specific 'benefits' or 'healing' of psychological and/or physical conditions are mentioned. The authors and publisher make no claim or take any legal responsibility for the effectiveness or benefits of reading this book, and deny all liability for any injuries or damages caused from following any suggestions made in this book or from contacting anyone listed in this book or its promotional materials.

ISBN-13: 978-0615471266
ISBN-10: 0615471269
LCCN: 2011905716
CBN Media New York, London

A GUIDE TO YOUR SUPREME POWER

CECIL SUWAL &
MARK BRENER

God created man in its own image and likeness
—Book of Genesis

...and no, man is not a fallen creature.

CONTENTS

INTRODUCTION
What This Guidebook Can Give You xiii

Prologue xxiii

PART I
Two Life-Changing Insights That Your Pastor or
Rabbi Never Told You 1

PART II
The Role Your Ego Plays in Determining
Your Success 17

PART III
Breakthroughs in Training Your Mind and
Brain for Power and Success 29

PART IV
Condition Your Genes So You Look
and Feel Half Your Age 41

PART V
Be Rich Forever: Maximizing Profits
in Investments and Stocks 55

PART VI
Profit in Global Markets: Leaders' New Patterns
of Thinking 69

PART VII
Eliminate Failure Forever: Transcend the
Two Most Limiting Beliefs .85

PART VIII
Unleash Your Winning Streak: Mastering
Adversarial Situations 103

PART IX
Fuel For Life: Super-Charge Your
Closest Relationships 119

PART X
If You Want to Be Happy (and Successful),
Don't Believe These Ideas 135

PART XI
Become Immortal: Increase Energy, Youth,
and Vibrancy 149

PART XII
What Every Great Leader and Statesman Knows 165

PART XIII
Transform Your Negative Emotions Into Assets 181

PART XIV
Inside Information On Islam, Christianity,
and Israel 195

PART XV
What We Need to Know to Create Our Lives
the Way We Want Them to Be. 211

Meditation
The Key to Retraining Your Mind for Happiness,
Success, and Joy 227

A GUIDE TO YOUR SUPREME POWER

INTRODUCTION

What This Guidebook Can Give You

The wave or trend that we represent is gaining momentum. Its rising power is pulsating through every aspect of our social and individual lives. Those who ride the wave's crest will benefit the most. Humanity is quickly moving forward and its most successful leaders are those who are courageous enough to evaluate their long-standing beliefs. These are the people who endeavor to understand how the world is structured—how it is guided. They are the people who desire to synchronize with and thereby influence the unseen, most powerful mechanisms of the universe to their advantage.

You now hold in your hands the key to creative power, joy, happiness, wealth, and all things good. *A Guide to Your Supreme Power* is a complete system for lasting achievement, enduring fulfillment, health, confidence, wealth, and happiness in all areas of life. It is one of the few resources designed for leaders and those who aim to achieve their best in all they do.

Scientifically demonstrable results of using the system in *A Guide to Your Supreme Power* include higher levels of financial wealth, happiness, intelligence, health, creative genius, and enormous achievement in all areas of life. Not only do you begin to achieve more, but you also cultivate the mindset that enables you to enjoy both the processes involved and your results. Carefully reading and understanding *A Guide to Your Supreme Power* gives you a tremendous advantage over the masses in life, work, and love.

By eliminating discontent or depression and helping you advantageously balance worry, stress, and anxiety, the knowledge in *A Guide to Your Supreme Power* saves you time, work, and money. It shows even the most successful achievers how to constructively channel their energy so that the greatest powers in the universe (both physical and spiritual) always unite to work in their favor.

A Guide to Your Supreme Power presents an especially empowering world view that unifies different religious groups and celebrates the world's cultures. Churches of all denominations and spiritual congregations have fervently been sharing *A Guide to Your Supreme Power* with their followers in what has become a newly successful effort to increase their congregations' levels of joy and spiritual growth.

Empowered readers everywhere are discussing *A Guide to Your Supreme Power* with loved ones and family members over dinners and at parties…The knowledge we presented here has begun to feverishly sweep through social networks as millions of friends online share, post, and repost what they've learned in this guidebook and how it has benefited their lives.

One-by-one people have been discussing how *A Guide to Your Supreme Power* has helped them realize their dream jobs, promote their careers, transform their businesses, ace tests in school, make new friends, find their soul mates, inhabit their ideal homes, and return tense family relations back to loving harmony. It has allowed people to obtain enormous financial freedom (even millions) while experiencing joy.

Just scanning *A Guide to Your Supreme Power* and its contents takes your thought paradigm to the next level. By doing the weekly exercises included at the end of each chapter, you catapult yourself to success beyond previous recognition. Thus, your life is made on your terms, according to your most glorious visions.

༄

It took us approximately fifteen years to compile the information in *A Guide to Your Supreme Power*. We read and examined over a thousand books and informative sources on science, spirituality, psychology, ancient wisdom, and religion. We tested and verified (in every step of life) the knowledge we so scrupulously acquired. This complete system, *A Guide to Your Supreme Power*, concisely presents the most valuable information we found to date. It is the culmination of years of research, thought, practical implementation, mistakes, triumphs, and...profound discovery.

If you are skeptical that this system will advance and improve any aspect of your life, we especially welcome you to read it. We know that when skeptics advocate this system—based on personal example and their own achievements—the effect is considerable. And, bottom line, we want you to succeed. We want you to be our emissary. For skeptics, believers, and anyone else who is serious about maximizing the joy of life, this system *works*.

Even before fully clarifying the components of this thought system, we created and managed an international, multi-million-dollar venture. During that time we had sufficient wealth and each others' love...yet we were somewhat preoccupied with the idea that "something" wasn't quite complete. We just weren't as routinely happy, peaceful, or fulfilled as we expected we would be, given our circumstances.

Then the answer came. Indeed the knowledge in *A Guide to Your Supreme Power* was solidified and finely tailored only *after* we were given a most unique life and business challenge. Due to a series of sensational events associated with New York Governor Eliot Spitzer's resignation and our company at the time, *Emperors Club*, we were separated from each other...then our business was closed, *and* we

INTRODUCTION

were imprisoned. Having lost nearly everything (except each other in spirit and our families) we underwent massive psychological pain. We emotionally and spiritually grew up. What was our lowest point in life became our most profound turning point.

Viewing these past events as a catalyst for growth, we took these challenges and decided to learn from them. We focused our efforts on understanding just how this world works and why things happen as they do. We soon felt a deep stirring within—a burning desire—to share the extensive knowledge we acquired during this time and over the past fifteen years with as many people as possible. It would inevitably lead to happier, more fulfilling lives for everyone.

Thus, a new chapter opened for us. With the ways that this universe works, you now hold in your hands the key to creative power, joy, happiness, wealth, and all things good.

෴

You're warned not to attempt to read this book as though it were a novel. The knowledge contained in *A Guide to Your Supreme Power* is often quite deep (and scientific in nature). Each chapter should be read and re-read so its full meaning can be fully grasped and internalized. In this way the real value of *A Guide to Your Supreme Power* is gained.

Indeed, each chapter in and of itself contains essential components for acquiring real power. As you begin to understand each component in its entirety, you move closer toward being able to live the life you've always wanted to live...toward being able to have what you've always wanted to have. But again, attempting to read *A Guide to Your Supreme Power* as though it were a novel would be little more than a waste of time and money.

A Guide to Your Supreme Power begins by discussing the two core premises from which constructive, powerful thought is born. It then reveals how the mind and brain work together—and how to train their processes and mechanisms for your advantage.

We then disclose key principles for maintaining perfect health, high energy, confidence, and youthful vigor. (These principles alone can help you work miracles... from relieving chronic pain, depression, and anxiety to permanently recovering from illness and disease).

We continue to guide you toward enormous wealth and success by sharing techniques for accessing the best consultant in finance and business. *A Guide to Your Supreme Power* then reveals the power and beauty of close relationships (and how to effectively cultivate them). We also show you the ways to train your emotions so they naturally work in your favor...and much, much more.

INTRODUCTION

You will notice that throughout *A Guide to Your Supreme Power* we shed new light on long-held beliefs that permeate our society and grossly limit people's current ways of thinking. There is enormous creative power in this.

You may find that the ideas in *A Guide to Your Supreme Power* sometimes defy your current way of thinking. This just means you're on the right track. To advance yourself you must step out of your box of comfort and think differently than most of the crowd. You should act from a more advanced, more powerful, more creative mind-set if you are to secure greater, more satisfying results than ever before.

After reading just the first few pages of *A Guide to Your Supreme Power*, your perspective and inner vision expand to better serve you. Doing just a few minutes of the exercises at the end of each chapter increases the speed and magnitude of positive change. The exercises are meant to be done on a weekly basis, but feel free to read past each exercise to the next part, as you like. You can always return to the initial exercises with even greater insight than before. But *definitely do* the exercises each week...

However, you're cautioned not to proceed with reading the next chapters until you've understood the knowledge shared in the previous parts. Otherwise, the information that follows may not be fully understood which means that its benefits cannot be experienced.

Given that *A Guide to Your Supreme Power* touches on many important facets of reality and life, you may find yourself switching back and forth between chapters, according to your individual needs, goals, dilemmas, or desires at any given time. This system is cohesive and powerful, so please utilize it as you feel most comfortable. We should mention that this system does not include hypnosis or subliminal messages. Interestingly enough, many of the exercises may activate some of the same mechanisms as hypnosis—but we grant the power of influence over your own mind to you.

The difference between achieving success and failure, happiness and despondence, fulfillment and desire—is discussed in *A Guide to Your Supreme Power*. Indeed, the system in *A Guide to Your Supreme Power* can eliminate failure from any person's life. Even the most successful entrepreneurs, scientists, artists, politicians, athletes, and leaders have something invaluable to learn from *A Guide to Your Supreme Power*.

There is not a single thing that you can't do with this knowledge. Once you turn the page, you will have taken the first step toward guaranteeing your supreme power and happiness. Replace anxiety with confidence, stress with joy and take yourself to higher than ever before levels of: fulfillment, happiness, and financial reward. As you start to exude creativity and genuine happiness, you will look and feel more radiant and more powerful than ever.

It is our privilege to deliver *A Guide to Your Supreme Power*.

—CECIL "CECE" & MARK
Info@TheOneWorldInitiative.com
www.TheOneWorldInitiative.com
twitter.com/cecilandmark
facebook.com/markbrener.cecilsuwal

P.S. Before you continue reading please be sure to download your free companion pamphlet for *A Guide to Your Supreme Power* at: www.TheOneWorldInitiative.com/bookcompanion.html

P.P.S: As you're reading, if you have any questions about the contents of *A Guide to Your Supreme Power* please contact us via email Info@TheOneWorldInitiative.com

PROLOGUE

Change is the law of life. And those who look only to the past or present are certain to miss the future.

—John F. Kennedy

Before the act of creation everything was one. Everything was God and God was everything. A state of complete *monism* (where all things are one) existed.

With the act of creation there became two: God-Creator and its creation. This is what is meant by the term *dualism*. The act of creation signified a birth and evolvement of the universe.

As the book of Genesis states, "God created man in its own image and likeness." The act of creation is still in progress; humankind is evolving toward godlikeness. The act of creation appears very long to us humans (from thousands to billions of years, so far), but for an infinite God-Creator, the process is essentially instantaneous, as time relativity shows.

As the act of creation progresses, humans become more godlike. Advancement toward godlikeness grants us massive power to create our lives exactly as we want them to be. As we become more godlike, we join or unify with our God-Creator. In doing so, we emerge as co-creators. To be co-creator is to have free will and creative power absolutely equivalent to God, free of any human limitations.

As we humans grow toward godlikeness, two (Creator and creation) once again become one. This state of oneness that exists when humanity is fully godlike is different than the initial state of oneness that existed prior to creation. It is a state of partnership or co-creation between the Creator and its human creation.

PART I

Two Life-Changing Insights That Your Pastor or Rabbi Never Told You

As humans we have an innate psychological tendency to look for beginnings and ends. That is the way the human brain and mind are designed. We tend to seek the truth of our origins or our purpose for being here on earth. When we realize our purpose, we come to understand the mechanisms of happiness and success.

Since the beginning of time as we know it, we have all been asking ourselves, "Where did we come from?" "Why are we here?" and "Where are we going?" *A Guide to Your Supreme Power* addresses these long-standing issues, creating what is the most empowering theory to date.

As Stephen Hawking correctly mentioned, there are hundreds of thousands of theories concerning human origin and purpose.[1] Some are theological and some are scientific. None are better or worse than the others. All theories are simply a product of people's abilities to interpret the world and their surroundings at a given time. In your quest for happiness and fulfillment you are ultimately free to choose whichever model of creation or origin you prefer.

Humanity's *current* ideas concerning the origins and destiny of the universe are intellectually incomplete and can therefore be misleading or psychologically weakening. To be clear, these current ideas originate from St. Augustine (one of the most important theologians), who saw the world as decaying. According to him, the world or universe emerged from a perfect beginning and was now moving toward a disastrous end. This was scientifically translated into what we now know as the Big Bang theory.[2]

There is substantial reason to believe that the universe is not in the process of decay as the Big Bang theory and St. Augustine propose. In fact, there is a model of the universe that both satisfies Einstein's equations and suggests perpetual growth or universal expansion, as opposed to decay.[3] Really, the Big Bang was likely just a small part of what is happening in our entire "super" universe. Even if a person accepts the Big Bang theory, the question remains: What happened *before* the Big Bang?...*and before that?*...*and before that?*...and so on.

Such inquiry inevitably leads to the concept of a primary entity that does not need to be created or caused. For communicative purposes in this system, we call this point of reference for human origin God-Creator.

You may know this ultimate creative power, God-Creator, under various names (universal consciousness, God, source energy, nature, spirituality, etc.) but the concept is the same. To align and harmonize yourself with this ultimate creative power you must know the principles underlying its operation. How it functions and how it directs the events in this world.

According to our model, *relative to human powers and abilities* (and as Creator), God is all mighty. Based on this, God-Creator should also be omni-loving (all loving), omnipresent (everywhere), and omniscient (all knowing).

The ultimate standard of success, therefore, is God-Creator. That is the entity that has all wealth, knowledge, love, beauty, health, happiness, joy, and all things good. To look to any other standard is to do yourself an impractical, *most limiting* disservice. When we look at Albert Einstein, Leonardo da Vinci, Johann Bach, and other enduringly influential people, it is fair to presume that they looked to God-Creator as their ultimate, inspirational source.

This chapter introduces you to God-Creator's power and, more importantly, to key aspects of God-Creator's design. It provides a foundation from which the design's mechanisms can be better understood—and utilized by those who wish to do so for their favor. Please note that accessing this power is by no means contingent on being religious or believing in a personal God.

After carefully reading and re-reading the chapters that follow and doing the exercises, you will have everything you need to fully align yourself with enormous creative power for your advantage. This enables you to create your life the way you want it to be: happier, more fulfilling, and entirely joyful...so you can have: your dream home, your perfect car, your ideal job, your soul mate....

But first, Part I.

PART I

1. There are two basic existential approaches to life. Both are legitimate but they differ in power. One approach sees the world through the assumption of chaos. The other approach sees the world through the recognition of order.

2. If you choose to accept the concept of chaos, all things result from random coincidence and should be analyzed from this fragmented perspective. If you choose to accept the idea of order, nothing is the result

of coincidence, and all things should be holistically evaluated accordingly.

3. The claim of chaos is due to a lack of understanding. It is a result of unfinished progress in science and philosophy. Mechanisms of the human body and our physical world were once deemed chaotic—until science began to unveil the precise order with which they function.

4. Incomplete knowledge regarding the intricate mechanisms of our environment and surroundings—of the structure of our world and life in general—is often written off as "chaos." Where we do not yet see order or coherence, it does not exist for us; but history shows that does not mean it does not exist at all (examples are modern medicine, physics, astronomy, etc.).

5. In fact, science continues to reveal the world as an intricately ordered mechanism. With the discovery and technological implementation of this order, things that were conceived of in science fiction just decades ago are now taken for granted as mundane reality.

6. Despite enormous progress in science and intellect, we humans still do not understand in full the structure or creation of the world. Of course we can and should use current scientific and what we call "spiritual" knowledge for our benefit. This is what some of the most prominent leaders in politics, science, art, and finance often do. To achieve enduring success you must harness

(rather than work against) the power of the laws of the universe.

7. Every scientific discovery reveals another aspect of the underlying order, the design, upon which our world rests. The existence of this order shows that the world is intelligently organized. There have always been advanced thinkers who used this design, these laws (biological, physical, spiritual, etc.), for their benefit and the benefit of humankind.

8. Still, the intricacies of the way that these universal laws interact surpass our current state of knowledge. They are beyond human scientific and intellectual abilities at this time.

9. Since human intellect and tools cannot yet decode the vast complexity of this lawful organization in full, it follows that there is a *higher* organizing power behind it, a power that is beyond us and our comprehension. We call this power God-Creator. Again, you may know this power under another name (universal consciousness, God, source energy, nature, etc.), but the concept is the same.

10. This creative organizing power, God-Creator, intelligently organizes everything. Relative to our human state of intellectual and spiritual evolution at this time, God-Creator is *all mighty*. To be all mighty is to be omnipotent, omnipresent, omniscient and omni-loving (it is important to remember that God-Creator's love is

of a different, far more comprehensive nature than what we call human love).

11. Since God-Creator is omnipotent, omnipresent, omniscient, and omni-loving, there is no place for any alternate power or force. You can think of the form "omni" metaphorically as a glass of water that is 100 percent full with no space remaining for anything else.

12. Speaking about the existence of a devil or evil as a separate entity therefore means detracting from the meaning of omni and thereby changing the definition of God-Creator to something else.

13. Wherever a person sees evil in another person or event, he or she lacks a fundamental understanding of God-Creator's design. Since God-Creator is omnipotent and pragmatically omni-loving, there can be no evil in its creation.

14. What someone calls evil is in reality a mental construct that is created when that person experiences pain (whether it is real, imagined, physical, or emotional). The idea of evil is designed to be a motivating force or catalyst; it drives humans away from that which is potentially destructive and toward that which is constructive.

15. Pain is not evil. It is a catalyst for change, development, and growth. God-Creator (the ultimate creative organizing power) intelligently organizes everything

toward godlikeness. To be godlike is to be creative, loving, powerful, successful, compassionate, wisely forgiving, and all things good. It includes having the wisdom to understand the complexities and intricacies of life. Development toward godlikeness is the ultimate purpose of creation and human existence. What we call pain is simply a prompt for growth toward greater godlikeness; it is an integral part of the design at this stage of human growth.

16. To better understand the concept of pain as a catalyst for growth, let's take an oversimplified example: think of an owner taking a pet dog or cat to the vet. The dog or cat is going to get vaccinations that could potentially save its life and protect it from illness or disease. What's happening is a *good* thing. Yet sometimes we see these pets crying (in emotional pain) as they're being transported to the vet...Like us humans, they are crying because they don't know or *understand* that what is going on is actually a good thing. They don't understand that what is happening will benefit them enormously. In their confusion and lack of knowledge, they experience emotional pain. This is similar to what happens to us humans when we experience pain.

17. Still, we humans interpret events as either painful or pleasurable. They are defined as evil or good. In reality (from the Creator's perspective) a world designed with omniscient omni-love can have no evil or good. We sim-

ply judge things as evil or good, depending on whether they are painful or pleasurable—and we judge pain and pleasure according to our interpretations of things.

18. When (according to the system explained in *A Guide to Your Supreme Power*) we interpret events and other people from the view that all things exist as a result of an omni-loving God-Creator, we begin to search for the benefits in *all* things. Our perspective becomes more godlike. We come to realize that the concepts evil and good exist only in human thought and perception. These ideas (evil and good) are psychological responses, relative mental interpretations of stimuli. They are catalysts or motivating forces in our growth.

19. In a world created by an omnipotent and omni-loving God-Creator, every event serves both God-Creator and its creation. All is purpose-driven. In this creation, nothing can be evil.

20. The term evil was once an essential idea but is now an outdated relic from our earlier stages of evolutionary creation (the human journey toward godlikeness). It is a result of incomplete knowledge of the intricate mechanisms that structure our world, incomplete knowledge of ourselves and of God-Creator.

21. Since an omnipotent and pragmatically omni-loving God-Creator created the world, good and evil cannot battle for your soul or for anything else. All things occur

to foster your greatest growth toward godlikeness (creativity, joy, love, etc.).

22. The words "good" and "evil" have relative meanings. Some things that were once perceived by some people as good (for instance the Spanish Inquisition) are no longer perceived this way and vice-versa. The concepts of evil and good are directly derived from a person's experience of pain and pleasure. What a person thinks is excessively painful is deemed evil, and those things we find pleasurable are good.

23. Pain and pleasure depend on the way we interpret our sensory perceptions. These mental interpretations affect our minds, brains, and whole nervous systems.

24. By changing our mental interpretation of a thing, it gains different meanings and affects us differently. Depending on how we interpret pain, it can be a building block or a road block. Where our interpretations are favorable, they serve us; we evolve toward greater godlikeness.

25. Pain and pleasure are therefore basic tools in divine management. This refers to the way by which God-Creator prompts the perfect development of its creation. Since God-Creator has created us, all intricacies of individual human psychology and thought should be seen as sophisticated mechanisms in divine management. Though, clearly we humans have evolved to have free

will. The more we evolve toward godlikeness the more free will we gain (see PART XV for more on free will and how we can increase it in our lives).

26. Realizing the existence of God-Creator as omnipotent, omnipresent, omniscient, and omni-loving—and interpreting incoming stimuli via this perspective—aligns you with this ultimate power in every way. You begin to reflect and attune to this power. This power grants you things like the freedom and finances to travel at whim, the ability to develop the career of your dreams, so you can buy and have anything that you want at any moment...to live the life of your dreams.

27. The Bible states, "God created man in its own image and likeness." This means that God created humans as perfect entities (from God-Creator's perspective) with power second to God-Creator's. The main component of this power is the power of creation. We have only to evolve to reach our full potential, to become more godlike. Even the smallest step toward godlikeness endows us with enormous creative power...*A Guide to Your Supreme Power* provides direction.

28. It is important to remember that God-Creator's act of creation is still in progress. This is what is meant by the term "evolutionary creation." Due to time relativity, what appears to be thousands of years for a human is mere "seconds" for an infinite, all-powerful God-Creator.

29. Your life is part of the creation toward godlikeness, toward the power for godlike creation. Our bodies, as part of God-Creator's creation, consist of trillions of law-driven cells. The nucleus (or center) of each cell contains the DNA that comprises our genetic makeup. Our DNA contains the instructions that direct our bodies' cells; it is a storehouse of information.[4]

30. The brain is also a storehouse of information. It is comprised of billions of cells called neurons that exchange information. Given the brain's vast capabilities, some of the most knowledgeable neuroscientists and Nobel Prize laureates once stated that as little as 3–4 percent of the human brain is actually utilized. While many now confirm that the entire brain is indeed being used, it is unlikely that humans have evolved to reach their full intellectual capacity.

31. As we grow more godlike, the human brain develops more highly, and our current abilities increase. Progress in evolutionary creation (the human journey toward godlikeness) is required for this development.

32. As humans progress, so do the sensory stimuli in our surroundings. With the onslaught of advertisements, cell phones, and social media the brain is now exposed to trillions of bits of sensory information each day. Only the information that we recognize registers with our minds. The rest of the stimuli go unnoticed and are not processed by our brains.

33. The things on which you tend to focus determine the sensory stimuli that your mind and brain recognize. What you tend to focus on is influenced by your general perspective of the world. The things you focus on signify your level of growth and development, as does the way you perceive and interpret reality. To evolve toward godlikeness, it is imperative that you consciously and constructively guide your focus.

34. *A Guide to Your Supreme Power* is designed to increase your level of godlikeness and your personal power and ability to create your ideal life. It will show you how to activate the storehouses of creative intelligence that reside dormant within you. Awakening this intelligence by a mere fraction of a percent catapults you to an entirely different plane of human existence. It massively increases your human power and ability to create in any field (financial, personal, business, etc.). It brings you closer to being godlike.

35. By viewing reality through the empowering perspective, as outlined in *A Guide to Your Supreme Power*, and using meditation to train your mind (which is a form of neuroscientific mind training), you unlock enormous creative power for our human needs, similar to God-Creator. As the Bible states, "God created man in its image and likeness."

36. All that we need to reach the highest possible levels of godlikeness is here. Physics has just begun to unveil this. The most irreducible form of matter known to us,

so far, is actually consciousness or "information." Our immediate senses do not absorb this information and the information of even more subtle fields; it can, however, be accessed during contemplation and meditation. This is when the senses and thoughts are quieted, which makes it the easiest way to access empowering, constructive, and creative information pertinent to your causes.

37. Via quieting the senses and thoughts during contemplative meditation, your brain is empowered, which gives you the ability to control your focus. Remember, your habitual focus determines the sensory stimuli that your mind and brain recognize and process.

38. Since your beliefs and preconceptions determine the external information that is accessible to your mind and brain, it is imperative that you realize two major points mentioned in this chapter. These are the two key premises that breed empowerment.

39. The first (you don't have to be religious) is that this universe is intelligently organized. It is not chaotic but, as leading science continues to confirm, is comprised of precise, intricate order or design, implemented by a higher intelligence, which we call in *A Guide to Your Supreme Power*, God-Creator.

40. The second important point is that God-Creator is: omnipotent, omnipresent, omniscient, and omni-loving. As with any creator, God-Creator has every interest in

the absolute success of its creation, which includes you as well.

41. For your exercise this week, take a seat in a quiet place where you feel comfortable and safe and where it is unlikely that you will be disturbed. Close your eyes; allow your mind to absorb and analyze this chapter's information on the conscious and subconscious levels. Do this at some point each day (approximately fifteen to twenty minutes each day). Begin to interpret all that you see, hear, witness, and experience from the perspective that the world was intelligently designed by an omni-loving God-Creator.

The whole history of science has been the gradual realization that events do not happen in an arbitrary manner, but that they reflect a certain underlying order, which may or may not be divinely inspired.
—STEPHEN HAWKING

PART II

The Role Your Ego Plays in Determining Your Success

All aspects of your being should function in balance. This is how you come to reflect and therefore gain the power and support of God-Creator's design. To be perfectly balanced, the aspects of your mind must be balanced as well. This includes the ego.

The ego (when balanced) serves a vital role in the human mind or it would not exist. In fact, all of the information that you encounter in life is transformed by your mind and brain into coherent ideas based on your existing beliefs, or your ego. When the ego is balanced, this mechanism is advantageous.

However, if the ego were to transform into a reflexive thought-mechanism that prevented you from acquiring new information or experiencing life in new ways, you'd want to know about it. You'd want to learn its unbalanced mechanisms so you could observe and better control them. You'd want to retrain these mechanisms to serve you rather than work against you, as it does for so many people...

For example, the human tendency is to simply interpret new stimuli in a way that enables people to confirm what they already "know" and believe. This is called "confirmation bias"[1] and is not a creative mode of thought. Research shows that the more a person can retrain his or her mind to resist confirmation bias, the more that person gains financially.[2]

This chapter helps you discover the ego's most unconstructive mechanisms. It helps you recognize and retrain them for your advantage (financial, interpersonal, and more). While many people routinely function on egocentric "auto-pilot," no person of creative power would allow such mindlessness to dominate his or her thoughts. And if you are to truly advance, grow happier, and become more joyously fulfilled, neither can you... Understanding the egoic mechanisms presented in this chapter gives you an unbelievable short-cut to living the life of your dreams.

And now, Part II.

PART II

1. Most people hardly ever conceive of anything new. They reprocess the same thoughts, beliefs, and information over and over, sometimes with a slight variation.

2. Original external stimuli and new knowledge are thus interpreted and processed according to the same repetitive ideas. These ideas are comprised of what the person already thinks he or she knows and believes about him/herself, others, and the world in general.[3]

3. It is known that consistent thinking breeds consistent action and consistent results. While a person may be generally pleased with the results of his or her thoughts and behavior until now, he or she will always desire new, better, more successful, creative, or influential outcomes. The expansive law of the universe indicates that what is not actively advancing is actively falling behind. This is true in business, science, and all human development.

4. Many people think they are advancing, but they are not. They are merely recreating the same circumstances with "commendable" precision—as opposed to growing, advancing.

5. The redundant thought mechanisms that produce a sense of comforting pleasure or certainty in life are the same thought mechanisms that limit you from

producing greater levels of happiness for yourself and your family.

6. If you do not consistently enrich your mind with leading knowledge and information, it is impossible to advance further than your current situation. If you do not challenge your consistent perspectives and consider completely original ways of perceiving the same reality, your situation will always be stagnant—and therefore limited.

7. It is not "reality" that changes or grows but our knowledge and perceptions of it. Frontier science has not "created" anything new in this world. It has uncovered what has always been. This is always done following original and new perceptions of reality—insight. They are the founts of creative power. And having creative power means being able to reach all of your goals. Having creative power means being able to make more money in more innovative ways. It means freedom.

8. When the personality's ego becomes too large, it is impossible to exercise original insight in any endeavor. Creative power is restricted.

9. It is the individual's ego that contains all the fixed ideas a person has about him or herself and the world. It serves as a necessary reference point for human functioning and interpretation.[4] The ego must be kept in balance

or retrained if it is to serve its most beneficial functions without incurring adverse effects.

10. It is known that one must have a stable sense of self to optimally function in the world. However, when the number of rigidly fixed ideas a person has is too great, he or she cannot interpret incoming stimuli in new, rewarding ways. Instead, all things are judged as either meeting his or her preexisting requirements or not.

11. In a universe designed by an omni-loving, omnipotent, omniscient God-Creator, all things are beneficial. The basic mechanisms of your ego serve a positive purpose: to orient you in the world.[5] The ego enables you to interpret reality using core assumptions—about yourself, your identity, and the world in general. It provides a sense of continuity and order in the mind, a coherent sense of self.

12. It is only when the ego becomes too large or inflated that genuine creative power is sacrificed for an arrogant sense of already knowing. It is impossible to perceive or conceive of anything new (and equally rewarding) under such circumstances.

13. When the ego is unbalanced, or too large, the mind processes information homogeneously. Knowledge, people, and events are interpreted using the same core judgments and assumptions. The ego crudely filters the input, as opposed to allowing the mind to plausibly decode it.

14. While many assumptions contained by the ego may be correct, its body of ideas is ultimately small (and therefore limiting). Under the guidance of an overactive ego, people will apply essentially accurate knowledge to situations in which *that* knowledge doesn't pertain.[6] You cannot creatively or powerfully function in the world using a handful of fixed assumptions.

15. When you recognize that all things function according to basic laws (that science continues to unveil), you have no need to cling tenaciously to the few egocentric assumptions that provide you with "certainty." *A Guide to Your Supreme Power* discusses the most basic laws upon which the universe functions. Such knowledge enables you to step out of your "ego box" and operate from a much larger, more powerful understanding of reality.

16. When a person is in his or her ego box, incoming stimuli are interpreted in ways that fit the ego's existing beliefs. If incoming information contradicts one of the few ideas the ego has, the person outright rejects the information as inaccurate or simply discredits the source of the information.[7] Newness and creativity are inhibited. Negative emotions flood the body's cells and nervous system.

17. These egocentric mechanisms occur below the level of explicit consciousness. Simply knowing how they work cultivates greater awareness. This allows you to expand your mind to think beyond basic thought reflexes.

18. Immediate floods of anger, resentment, arrogance, or generally negative feelings toward the information or its source often accompany egocentric reflexes. The more frequently this happens, the more imbalanced the ego is, and the less one is aligned with God-Creator's design and its inherent power.

19. In a world created by an omnipotent, omni-loving God-Creator, all things serve a positive purpose (including the need to balance the ego). When balanced, the ego serves as a motivating force that increases our levels of effort. This is accompanied by improved performance on cognitive or attentional tasks.[8]

20. All aspects of God-Creator's design require balance. When the ego is excessively unbalanced, no benefits accrue. Indeed, it takes much more mental effort to interpret incoming stimuli *through* the ego—and increased performance does not constantly result from this increased effort.[9] This means that a person is not synchronized with the power of God-Creator's design.

21. As far as the ego is concerned, great arrogance is as unconstructive as excessive insecurity.[10] They both result in misinterpretations of reality and reduce creative genius. A person who thinks too highly of him or herself is prone to the same amount and degree of error as the person who cannot muster the faith in him/herself or reality to act.

22. God-Creator's design is such that you cannot affect one aspect of the design without affecting all others. All aspects of your being are synchronized just as all aspects of God-Creator's design act in coherent unison. Imbalanced thought mechanisms create physical imbalances at the cellular level.

23. High ego involvement is shown to increase systolic and diastolic blood pressure and heart rate.[11] When a person equates his or her level of self-worth with a given task or goal, the ego is active— mental effort and performance *might* improve.[12] For this to occur, blood pressure and heart rate rise. Despite these physical changes, increased performance is not always assured.[13] Clearly, the ego serves a vital purpose for success and development in God-Creator's design, but must be balanced to gain its precarious benefits.

24. Imbalance usually arises when the ego or sense of self becomes over-active. In such instances nearly all that a person attempts to accomplish defines his or her perceived self-worth. Indeed, in some cases this is actually a manifestation of insecurity. The person assumes that he or she has no value, unless he or she can associate him/herself with the eventual accomplishment of his or her goals. Despite the insecurity it attempts to conceal, this is a manifestation of high ego involvement.

25. With consistently high egocentric involvement, all things are rigorously interpreted based on a relatively few fixed ideas of how things "should be." Anxiety, anger, worry, and stress replace the naturally flexible, inquisitive, creative genius within. A desire to explore the principles of creation diminishes. In time the physical coherence of one's body reflects this highly egocentric mental state.

26. It is known that mental incoherence soon disassembles physical coherence. Anxiety, stress, anger, and other extreme emotional states that characterize ego imbalance interfere with immunity and physical strength. This results in countless potential illnesses, such as hypertension, heart disease, thyroid disease, cancer, etc.[14]

27. In a world designed by a pragmatically omni-loving, purpose-driven God-Creator, all things serve a beneficial purpose. When ego imbalance prompts cellular incoherence, any potentially resultant illness is merely a catalyst for growth. It helps to further a person's knowledge and understanding of God-Creator's design—to cohesively align with God-Creator's power.

28. Sometimes an overactive ego causes a person to think that all things occur because of him or her. Because of this people may feel responsible for their illnesses or for causing the illnesses of those they love. It is important

to remember that all things are purposefully driven by an omni-loving God-Creator's design toward ultimate benefit and growth for all. This includes such things as physical illness and its eventual balancing.

29. Retraining the ego elicits perceptual balance and health. A properly balanced ego encourages creativity. When the ego is trained for balance it serves its most constructive functions, as intended by design, without incurring adverse effects, such as self-blame in the case of illness or the more frequent ego-shock in daily life.

30. Research shows that when the ego feels threatened, it throws the person's mental and physical system into a state of shock. This is known as ego-shock.[15] Indeed, a person's ego is threatened much more often than you might initially expect.

31. Ego-shock occurs any time basic external stimuli or newly presented knowledge does not quite correspond with the ideas and beliefs that a person already holds. Prior to discrediting the source or the actual knowledge itself,[16] the ego causes the person's mental system to briefly enter a state of internal shock.

32. During states of ego-shock, people cannot think clearly. Accurate perceptions of reality are temporarily suspended. This mentally paralyzing process is so brief that it often takes place without cognitive comprehension.[17]

33. The ego-shock process is automatic. It immediately results in a flood-like release of painful emotions like anger, sadness, confusion, and other unconstructive emotional states.[18] These are the states (even when mild) that prompt the ego to reject that which it initially, unconsciously perceived as threatening.

34. The ego considers stimuli threatening whenever the stimuli do not correspond with the ego's currently fixed ideas and beliefs. However, the number of ideas and beliefs that the ego has are very few in total—especially when considering the abundance of information that surrounds us. This means that *most* information is rejected by the ego (often unconsciously). It is not allowed into the mind for more comprehensive processing.

35. Immediately judging and then rejecting the information that one is presented with does not serve a person. It limits that which the mind can ultimately absorb and further process. A limited mind can create only equally limited conditions. Where the ego is over-active or under-active, growth is suspended.

36. This week try to monitor and observe your ego as it currently functions. You may be astounded (as most people initially are) at the amount of knowledge, information, and insight it routinely prevents your mind from absorbing. Constantly rejecting stimuli that do not

correspond to the ego's fixed preconceptions severely limits creative genius. The mind simply has fewer ideas to work with.

37. Imbalanced ego-activation causes many people to regress, as nothing remains fixed in an ever-evolving world. If you are to advance in power, you must be sure that your ego is trained to serve you.

38. To retrain the ego, go into the silence as you did last week. Contemplate and then meditate upon the knowledge presented herein. Allow the mind to use this knowledge to sow the seeds for enhanced insight and awareness of the ego's mechanisms. This will make it easier for you to notice any potentially unbalanced ego reactions throughout the next few days.

39. Via increased observation and awareness, you begin to retrain your ego to serve its most valuable functions but no more. You are on the way to cultivating greater creative genius. However, to do so, it is necessary to break any unconstructive egocentric reflexes that currently prevent new knowledge from entering your mind.

Common sense is the collection of prejudices acquired by age eighteen.
—ALBERT EINSTEIN

PART III

Breakthroughs in Training Your Mind and Brain for Power and Success

Acquiring new knowledge is important. A constructive perspective is equally, if not more, important. A constructive perspective elicits harmoniously constructive chemical processes in the brain. By training the content of your mind to be constructive in nature, you empower your brain—you elicit greater happiness, fulfillment, and success.

Your brain thinks in terms of patterns. It filters incoming stimuli according to the information it already contains. Anything that your brain does not recognize based on its existing network patterns is overlooked.[1] Thus, some of the most unique opportunities pass unnoticed.

Creating new levels of wealth, happiness, and fulfillment requires expanding your current thought patterns. The only way to expand your current thought patterns (and eliminate currently negative thought patterns) is to acquire new knowledge. By acquiring new knowledge you enrich and empower your existing knowledge. You develop greater insight and open your mind to new and higher levels of creative achievement. This means greater success, being able to live the life of your dreams, and obviously, having more money.

Thus, any new knowledge that you acquire should serve you. It should expand your thought paradigm for the better. It should support your brain in a chemically favorable way. It should reinforce and expand your power and creativity. The knowledge contained in this chapter is designed for this purpose.

PART III

1. The structure of the brain is intricate but certainly not beyond anyone's comprehension. For the purposes of this chapter, we present only the information most pertinent to wealth, happiness, and genuine fulfillment.

2. The human brain is comprised of billions of cells called neurons. These neurons communicate with each other via electrical signals. New neurons are born in your brain throughout your life via neurogenesis—this is the

process by which new neurons grow from the stem cells in the brain. Under normal circumstances our brains do not decay or weaken with age...unless we allow them to.

3. The general structure and functioning of the brain is better understood today than ever before—but far more remains to be discovered. For scientists the mind continues to be an even greater enigma than the brain. As humans grow toward godlikeness, during the course of evolutionary creation (the human journey toward godlikeness), our collective understanding of the mind and brain will increase.

4. According to current science, the mind is best described as the consciousness that includes our thought patterns, which are based on (and include) perception, memory, emotion, and imagination. The mind is the flux of all conscious and unconscious cognitive processes.

5. Your mind and brain are intimately connected, constantly affecting and influencing each other. By training the content of your mind, you empower your brain. This chapter shows you how it works.

6. Your individual thoughts and your consistent thought patterns determine the chemicals (neurotransmitters) secreted by your brain. Your thought patterns therefore directly influence the chemistry of your brain.

7. The neurons in your brain become accustomed to the chemicals that are habitually secreted by your brain

as a result of the thoughts that you have. Even negative thought patterns are "addictive" for neurons because neurons become chemically dependent on the chemicals most often secreted—good or bad.[2]

8. This basic nature of chemical addiction in the brain is most clear when considering outside chemicals being released into the brain—such as caffeine, for example. The same dependency occurs with the chemicals naturally released into and by your brain.

9. Retraining your mind can change *any* negative or unuseful thought patterns to which your brain is addicted. By strengthening the nature of your thoughts (the mind), you empower the neural structure of your brain. Your brain then influences the thought patterns of your mind based on its new, stronger, more optimistic neural structure and vice versa. A cycle of higher strength and power is perpetuated.

10. The chemicals released by stress kill the brain's neurons. Stress-induced chemicals destroy the brain's synapses. (Synapses are the small spaces between neurons that allow neurons to communicate with each other.) Stress also interferes with neurogenesis, which is the process by which new neurons grow from stem cells in the brain.[3] This means that stress reduces the cohesive structure of a person's brain and prevents new neurons from being born.

11. Consistent stress perpetuates a cycle of negative thought patterns since the mind and brain act cyclically upon each other. As a consequence stress inhibits constructive thinking and, therefore, creativity.

12. Creativity is the ability to unite seemingly contrasting facts and ideas. It is one of the greatest foundations of success and without it no one can prosper. Creativity is money and money is freedom. Freedom to travel, to buy the things you desire, to live in the home of your dreams...

13. A person's creativity is directly contingent on maintaining a cohesively structured brain. By killing neurons and synapses and preventing new neurons from growing, stress interferes with a person's brain structure. Creativity is inhibited, if not eliminated, by stress-induced chemicals. Stress must therefore be balanced to ensure consistently peak levels of constructive thought and creativity. To balance stress we should first understand it.

14. Stress is a result of the way you interpret events. Your focus and perception determine your interpretation.

15. When your core existential belief system serves you, you interpret events favorably. This strengthens the structure of your brain. Your brain begins to influence

your mind and thought patterns more favorably. In this way excess stress is eliminated.

16. Real changes are made only by conditioning and rewiring the mind to utilize a cohesive existential belief system. Any other changes may be helpful but superficial. They are therefore prone to error or weakness—during times that we need strength and creative power the most.

17. Any mental retraining other than the full internalization of a rational, credible, cohesive, existential belief system will falter when you need it the most. Consistent optimism is pleasant enough, but when things are challenging, nothing will sustain power and drive like a solid existential belief system—a belief system so intimately connected with true power that it can be used to calmly "whistle your way" through something as drastic as a prison term or the death of your spouse.

18. While the two above examples are interpreted by the mind as unpleasant or painful, you should begin to recognize that in a world created by an omni-loving, omniscient, and omnipresent God-Creator, everything is designed for a person's benefit and growth toward god-likeness. God-Creator is interested in each person's success and does everything for your (and others') benefit, because it is in God's own interest. This is God's omni-love. God-Creator has every interest in its creation reaching full completion.

19. An obvious expression of God-Creator's omni-love is the fact that human brain capacity is enriched by new experiences. Positive, new, experiences lead to new neurons being created in the brain and additional network connections being formed.[4] The power of your mind and brain increase with new and meaningfully positive experiences.

20. Many people have analogous experiences, but only a portion of them interpret the experiences positively or meaningfully. A negatively interpreted experience alters brain chemistry and structure, predisposing us (chemically and structurally) to future negative interpretations.

21. Our mind is exposed to four hundred billion bits of information per second. Of this four hundred billion, we process only two thousand bits.[5] The two thousand bits that your mind processes depends on your focus and perception.

22. Your focus and perception determine the quality of your experiences. Based on these you interpret your experiences to be pleasant or painful, positive or negative. Your focus at each given moment is determined by your existential belief system. Those who do not have a clear existential belief system function according to one that is simply incoherent or unstructured, the results of which can be confusing or disharmonious.

23. When your core existential belief system serves you, you interpret events favorably. This empowers your brain (structure and chemistry). Your brain then begins to influence your mind's thought patterns more favorably, which fosters an empowering, cyclical process.

24. To live a life of success, happiness, and true fulfillment is to first retrain your mind: to adopt a cohesive understanding of the world and its order. Realizing the fundamental order of this world prevents chaotic thought patterns (and the unconstructive biochemicals they produce). You will find that chaotic thought tendencies are the primary cause of many disagreeable conditions in life.

25. Think of the way the universe is structured—designed by an omni-loving Creator that wants the most and best for you. Your ultimate joy, happiness, and wealth are in God-Creator's interest. Try to interpret all outcomes (both "good" and "bad") from this perspective. Your personal experience may show that many things you once considered good were later seen as not so good and vice versa.

26. An omni-loving God-Creator designs the world according to basic physical and spiritual laws. Science continues to uncover these laws each day…what we know now was not always known. Much of what humans once believed would now be classified as primitive. Many things that we believe today will one day seem primitive as well.

27. As mentioned in Part I, Nobel Prize laureates once stated that, as little as 3–4 percent of the human brain is actually utilized. Neuroscience now asserts that we use the brain in its entirety. Perhaps both notions contain accuracy. While there is evidence suggesting that we currently use all of our brain's physical capacity, we are not yet using its full potential. This is the nature of evolutionary creation—we acquire more knowledge as we progress on our human journey toward godlikeness. Our brains evolve accordingly.

28. While the mind's influence on the brain's structure has been discovered, science has yet to finely pinpoint the origin of thought. Much remains to be learned about how the brain enables the mind to create what we call "consciousness." It is known that the mind's activity can either empower or weaken the coherent functioning of the brain.[6] However, you can systematically direct your conscious thoughts for your benefit.

29. You should therefore search for the benefits and advantages in all things. Sometimes the benefits in a situation will be apparent, and other times they may be veiled beneath the surface; but the rule is always the same.

30. It is in God-Creator's interest that you develop, grow, and advance. All things stem from an omni-loving God-Creator—and every occurrence should be interpreted

from this view (the advantages of this view are experienced, even if you are not "religious"). When everything is seen from this perspective, your thoughts and actions reflect this. You search for (and find) the benefits in all things; your fulfillment and success are assured.

31. To internalize this you must retrain your mind. The best tool for this is meditation. The best meditation known to us is TM (see the meditation section at the end of *A Guide to Your Supreme Power* if you haven't already). Only during meditation are the thoughts quiet enough to allow the enclosed information to be easily absorbed and realized. When your thoughts are quiet, you can open your mind (conscious and subconscious) to all powerfully transcendent information.

32. This week, meditate on the idea that an omni-loving, omniscient God-Creator designed the world. This God-Creator is interested in your success and does everything for your benefit—it is in God-Creator's interest. This will begin to influence your interpretations of the events you experience and your thought patterns. Your brain chemistry and structure will also positively change, according to this new realization. Harmony with the laws governing the universe increases. Happiness is certain.

33. When everything is seen from this perspective (that all things occur for your benefit and stem from an omni-loving God-Creator), you are activating a greater

coherence of thought from which to act and conduct your affairs.

34. In the next chapter, we will explain how this exercise can be expanded to activate a greater percentage of the intelligence that is dormant within you. This activation increases creative abilities, power, happiness, integrity, balance, and success.

35. But first, contemplate and then focus during meditation, when the mind is quiet, on the fact that everything (small and large) you encounter is designed by an omnipotent, pragmatically omni-loving God-Creator for both your and its benefit. Begin to search for these benefits each day.

36. Be sure to exit the meditative state slowly. As you are stepping out of the meditative state, tell yourself that you will feel excellent (no feelings of dizziness, nausea, or sleepiness). Once you are finished, give yourself five to seven minutes before you open your eyes and get up. Remember, like a deep ocean diver, you are moving from one state to the other. Do it slowly.

PART IV

Condition Your Genes So You Look and Feel Half Your Age

The science of epigenetics shows that we can alter the expression of our genes. Our habitual thoughts, perspectives, experiences, and lifestyle choices all influence the way our genes and cells express themselves.[1]

Where our habits are constructive, our gene expressions strengthen and serve us. Where they are not, genetic and cellular incoherence ensues. The results of cellular incoherence can range from basic energy loss to countless health-related problems. It is in a person's obvious interest to maintain cellular coherence: health.

This chapter contains a wealth of information from the fields of frontier science, nutrition, and health. It shows you how to activate the dormant creative intelligence within—catapulting yourself to even greater levels of success, while fostering perfect cellular health.

We have extracted the essence of that which is needed to secure full control of your physical health and make creative power your constant ally.

PART IV

1. That your happiness and success are contingent on the state of your health is an incontestable truth. Little is accomplished with low energy or a feeble mind or body.

2. Just as persistent thought-patterns produce chemical and structural changes in your brain, they create chemical and structural changes in every cell of your body. Accordingly, your mind's activity directly influences your immune system and determines your physical health.

3. The human body consists of trillions of cells. The nucleus of each cell contains the DNA that comprises your genetic makeup. It is known that creative intelligence lies dormant inside of us—even at these microscopic levels of our beings. We only need activate it.

4. Some of the highest financial elite, greatest scientists, artists, athletes, and intellectuals have likely activated a minute percentage of their additional intelligence. This chapter tells you how to activate your dormant creative intelligence to an even greater degree and achieve perfect health.

5. Every thought that you have produces a chemical reaction in your body. The cells of your body become habituated to the chemicals most often secreted as a result of your typical thought patterns. In this way, you maintain the unique cell structure of your body. Your cells are also habituated to any foreign chemicals you may consistently rely upon, such as caffeine or alcohol.

6. Each thought translates into a chemical reaction that affects every cell of your being. For example, thoughts of fear produce adrenaline. Excess adrenaline in the body creates fearful or stress-inducing thoughts. Consequently, the mind and body cyclically influence each other.

7. If your thoughts frequently lead to the secretion of adrenaline, the cells of your body become habituated to fear. Their tolerance for adrenaline increases. When this happens your cells come to crave fear, since they've grown so accustomed to adrenaline.

8. These and other consistent emotional or hormonal imbalances can prevent cells from receiving proper nutrition. This is because the receptor sites of the cells come to "want" the thought-induced chemicals most often released by the mind and body in lieu of genuine nutrition.[2] This phenomenon occurs whether these chemicals are constructive *or* damaging to health.

9. When you retrain your mind according to the principles enclosed in this chapter, you retrain the cells of your body—you secure perfect health and the creative power it generates. This means having a better life: more energy, all the money you need, and harmonious relationships.

10. Perfect health is not maintained unless the principles of a healthy life are understood and practiced. Activating the perfect intelligence of your being is impossible if your cells are not healthy, coherent, and fed with proper nutrition.

11. That food influences your cell structure is obvious. Your cells thrive on the nutrition that you feed them. Wholesome, healthy, nutritious food results in a coherent body of cells structured for perfect health. Cellular incoherence results from consuming unhealthy food. "Unhealthy food" is defined as food that is devoid of nutrition or has been chemically or structurally altered (in which case its structure is incoherent).

12. When you crave a specific food, it is likely a result of cellular imbalance. When balanced, your cells and body will guide you to the most nourishing food that is best for you. Of course a wealth of information on nutrition for health is available. Only you can fully implement the most beneficial health requirements for your unique lifestyle and makeup. (You can download free recipes from

gourmet, vegan-macrobiotic chefs, Eric Lechasseur and Sanae Suzuki, as well as a recipe from raw food, eco-chef, Bryan Au at: www.TheOneWorldInitiative.com/health-food.html).

13. To be a person of power, strength, and intelligent creativity, wholesome, nutritious eating habits are mandatory. So is constructive thought. Both the food we consume and our persistent thought patterns are interdependent and directly affect our cellular structures and health.

14. While health and nutrition influence the chemistry of the body, our thoughts and feelings also activate and deactivate our genomes. Genomes are the genetic material that comprises DNA. Stress, concern, and worry significantly alter cell structure by activating certain genomes and deactivating others.[3] Research shows that these and similar thought patterns, if persistent, contribute to illness and disease by inducing cell mutation.

15. Unconstructive thought patterns are the result of perception. The same conditions can be perceived as stressful for one person, neutral, or easily enjoyable for another. The difference in perception is caused by a difference in interpretation. When you recognize that all things result from the inherently benevolent design of an omnipotent, omni-loving God-Creator for your and its benefit, mental interpretations change. Thought patterns

expand to decipher the meanings, benefits, and opportunities in each situation. Stress is eliminated; opportunities are seized.

16. Some needless thought patterns are quite firmly (and unknowingly) ingrained in our minds and cell structure. For example, you will notice that people age at seemingly different paces. Some people appear quite old after just forty years, whereas others seem forty at the age of eighty. The differences result from lifestyle habits and a person's deep-seated thought patterns.

17. Once you fundamentally consider yourself old, your body follows. In this way your core thought processes influence your behavior and body by creating biochemical and structural changes in every cell of the body. As you think, so you are. Any thoughts pertaining to youth and health that do not serve you can be identified during meditation (they will surface). These and other disserving thought patterns are transformed when you retrain your mind in accordance with perfect health. Realizing the fully coherent perspective presented in *A Guide to Your Supreme Power* does this.

18. A coherent, empowering philosophy enables you to interpret situations for your benefit. A perception that consistently maintains your alignment with the highest power results in total happiness, success, and fulfillment. Your energy increases allowing you to vibrantly spend

more time doing the things you love with the people who matter most.

19. Once conditions and events are understood as having resulted from the omni-love of an omnipotent, omniscient God-Creator, you no longer experience stress. Undesirable thought patterns are replaced with empowering, loving, and optimistic thoughts. These thoughts improve immune system function,[4] creating a body of strength and vigor.

20. Your highest powers are realized upon understanding that this universe—and your physical being—are the designs of an omni-loving God-Creator. This God-Creator does everything for your benefit and, therefore, its own benefit. When fully realized and practiced, this outlook results in perfect mental and physical health. By understanding and focusing on the perfection of the design, you simultaneously facilitate perfectly coherent health—and perfect action. The perfection of God-Creator's design includes you and aspects of reality that may at times appear "imperfect"...as will be explained later.

21. When you know that all events and occurrences are unfolding in accordance with the perfect design of a loving God-Creator, potentially stressful events are understood as opportunities for growth. You begin to look for the benefits in all occurrences. Sometimes those benefits may not be readily apparent, but soon you find that all

things (good and bad) propel you forward on your journey toward godlikeness.

22. Circumstances that once elicited thought patterns to turn genomes on and off in ways that were unfavorable for you begin to do the opposite. Strength replaces weakness…when you search for the benefits in each situation—all given to you by an omni-loving God-Creator—you change your focus, which positively influences your cell structure. You gain control over the situation, thus becoming more godlike.

23. A superior focus results in new genome activation. Consistently positive perspectives reinforce constructive (potentially just activated) genomes. Simply reading this chapter has activated and deactivated certain genomes, making you that much stronger, as acquiring such knowledge has shown to do.[5]

24. Each time you understand Creation and God-Creator from the perspective outlined in *A Guide to Your Supreme Power*, you are retraining your mind for your benefit. Doing so closely aligns you with the greatest powers. You begin acting in accordance with the laws of the grand design, as opposed to against them. Alignment with these laws helps relieve chronic physical pain, anxiety, depression, and all forms of mental and physical disease.

25. God-Creator's omni-loving, omniscient design functions according to basic physical and spiritual laws of the universe. An understanding of these laws and total coherence with them increases a person's creativity (the ability to form solutions under pressure) and power.

26. By coming to know aspects of the design and its laws, you better understand God-Creator. This increases your creative abilities—your abilities to be godlike. Knowing the elements of the design's structure enables you to better influence its features for your and, therefore, God-Creator's benefit. Your physical body is part of the intricate design. Understanding the construction of your physical body is thus to your great advantage.

27. All of your thought patterns are biologically encoded. A coherent existential philosophy that is aligned with God-Creator's design results in a coherently encoded body of total strength. In such a body, illness cannot persist. Mutation that characterizes illness finds no subsistence in a perfectly coherent structure.

28. Each thought produces a corresponding array of chemicals in your body. Subtle cellular mutations that result in illness are sometimes created with negative, incoherent, or weakening thought patterns. Replacing potentially negative thought patterns with beneficial, highly constructive ones can reverse these mutations.

29. Constructive thought patterns release life-giving chemicals into your cells. Your cells respond to constructive mental activity by becoming habituated to the improved chemical environment in your body. In this way you are constantly remaking your body with your thought patterns and their related chemical components. Your existing cells and your new cells adapt to a physically powerful environment that facilitates health, strength, and well-being. A cycle of perfect health and power is perpetuated.

30. Almost every cell in the body is comprised of atoms that are no more than a single year old. Indeed, 98 percent of the atoms in our bodies are replaced with new ones annually.[6] These new atoms are conditioned into our existing bodies, according to our mental activity and the biochemicals that these mental activities release. Empowering perspectives create a powerful home for these new atoms. Consistently powerful thoughts leave no structural room for discordant illness.

31. Thus far, you have learned that you are recreating your body's cell structures at each moment, based on your thought patterns, the chemicals they release, and the food you consume. Use this knowledge to your benefit.

32. Even when someone is ill or suffers from a disease, this occurrence can be predesigned by a loving God-Creator for that person's ultimate advantage. It is an

opportunity to grow, learn, and become more godlike. Sometimes, illness enables a person to understand facets of this world that remain unknown to others. The ego may try to convince someone that being ill is his or her fault or that a loved one's sickness is his or her fault. This is never the case.

33. In a world of perfect order and design, created by a loving God-Creator, all things occur for your and God-Creator's benefit. When you fully realize this, you retrain your mind and cell structure for perfect health, happiness, fulfillment, and creativity.

34. When you retrain your mind in accordance with the principles in *A Guide to Your Supreme Power*, your body's cells will follow. Even the healing of potential illness or disease occurs exactly when it is to a person's highest benefit. A coherent mind mirrors God-Creator's coherent design. The result, when it is to your chief advantage, is a physically coherent cell structure.

35. Your body is naturally structured for perfect coherence, power, and health; your cells contain energy that is wrought with creative power. To delineate: Science has shown that DNA contains a person's genomes (genes). Inside DNA and its genomes are atoms. Inside these atoms are subatomic particles. Inside these subatomic particles there is space. This space is part of the quantum field.[7] This is the closest known field to true creative

intelligence or power. It is not only outside your body but also inside your DNA.

36. The space that quantum science locates inside of your DNA is not empty space. It contains subtle yet enormously powerful energy; the subtler the energy field, the more powerful is the energy in that field.[8] In just a single cubic centimeter of quantum space, there is more energy than is contained in all the matter of the universe.[9] The power available at the quantum level of our universe contains the greatest amount of influential energy known to humans, so far.

37. The quantum field is perceived by some people to be the closest (currently known) field to creative intelligence. However, there are likely even more subtle fields that we have yet to discover.

38. To activate your dormant intelligence and create perfect health, you should access the quantum and *even more subtle fields* inside of your body. The way to access these fields is through contemplation followed by meditation. Only meditation quiets the senses sufficiently to enable access to the origins of creative intelligence.

39. During meditative silence the cells of your body align with the perfect coherence of the universe. As this alignment strengthens with repetitive practice, *dis-ease* is impossible.

40. Via the quantum field to *even more* subtle levels, your brain and body's dormant creative intelligence are activated with the mere hint of an intention. Here, your gene activation patterns and cell structure align with the coherence of the universe, creating perfect health.

41. When you enter these subtle, potent energy fields via meditative silence, you also dive into a deeper stratum of your subconscious mind. You more closely align with the realms of cause. This gives you enormous power to influence the world of effects—the realm that we see with our eyes and, therefore, the realm that we tend to be absorbed with the most.

42. All creative solutions, creative ideas, health, and power originate at the most subtle levels of reality. To attempt to create and activate a thing in this world without intentionally accessing these realms is to handle only the unresponsive world of effects—blindly ignoring all active cause.

43. This week, once again, go into the silence of meditation. During this time allow the cells of your body to cohesively align with the perfect order of the universe—of God-Creator's design. In this way your perfect health renews.

44. As you meditate know that as you align with God-Creator's design you are activating the potent creative

intelligence that lies dormant inside of you. For this activation to occur, your cells, genes, and biochemistry must correlate with the perfect order of the universe. As they do, your dormant intelligence awakens effortlessly. Your cells and body cease to expend energy resisting God-Creator's powerful coherence.

45. During your meditation allow your body and mind to perfectly connect with the order of God-Creator's design. Realize that you are aligning your entire being with the greatest power of the universe. Your thought, speech, and action will soon reflect this.

46. That the universe is designed for your and God-Creator's benefit will be more and more evident, as you realize the total coherence upon which this universe is built. The results of this alignment with God-Creator's power will begin appearing in all aspects of your life. You will notice an improvement in all that you encounter—the ease with which you function—and that everything occurs for your ultimate happiness and benefit. You will feel a new degree of fulfillment, happiness, and gratitude. For this to occur, perfect coherence with the grand design is directly required.

PART V

Be Rich Forever: Maximizing Profits in Investments and Stocks

An investor searching the Internet for information is exposed to over three billion pieces of relevant information regarding his or her investment. That which the investor ultimately focuses on is determined by his or her emotional state.[1]

A person's emotional state is largely influenced by his or her knowledge, namely, the perspectives encouraged by that knowledge. And even *all* human knowledge of a subject is often insufficient. The 2008 financial meltdown illustrates this well.

However, events such as the 2008 meltdown and other financial events of this kind ultimately help individual investors, hedge funds managers, and stock brokers make more money…when these events are filtered through the knowledge presented in *A Guide to Your Supreme Power*. Indeed, these events initiate human advancement and progress as a whole.

All progress—whether it's social or personal—is a basic part of evolutionary creation (our human journey toward godlikeness). High-impact, collective experiences such as the 2008 meltdown provide us with additional insight on how to more effectively manage and direct our personal financial affairs and the economy as a whole.

We gain much by remembering that the totality of human knowledge is still quite limited in our current stage of evolutionary creation. The most effective way to overcome the inevitable limitations of currently incomplete human knowledge is to access the omni-knowledge of the best consultant. This chapter shows you how.

PART V

1. Thousands of years ago, we "knew" that the earth was flat. Hundreds of years ago, no one would have comprehended the meaning of, for instance, a cellular phone. During these time periods, these beliefs were our reality—our absolute truths.

2. Today, cellular phones are used by nearly everyone. The earth is no longer assumed to be flat. Consider the

knowledge and devices that people will use thousands of years from now. These potentially high-impact contributions are what Nassim Nicholas Taleb calls "black swans."

3. The most recent financial crisis was clearly a black swan. These kinds of events carry extreme results and are highly improbable according to our current prediction models. It is only *after* black swans occur that the best financial experts attempt to understand and predict their future occurrences, using newly expanded prediction models.

4. Financial black swans have high impact, partly because investment and trading firms could not devise reliable and profitable models that could take into account black swan phenomena.[2] This exclusion-based methodology makes all of us (including these firms and their clients) vulnerable to the enormous losses that these events can elicit.[3]

5. Given the limitations of human intellect and prediction, there is only one steadfast way to flawlessly manage trading, investment, and business. You must take into account that which is not explicitly known.

6. Indeed, even the most advanced prediction models comprehend only a miniscule part of God-Creator's grand design. Limited to past-event-analysis, these

models reflect our current stage of evolutionary creation. With time (and human progress) prediction models become more advanced and much more intricate.

7. What we consider black swans today will be common knowledge in thousands of years; other black swans will appear in their places. Because of this process, the human prediction paradigm becomes more inclusive. Progress is made.

8. After a black swan, expert explanations concerning its cause abound. This is also the case with the most recent financial crisis. Many people attribute the event to various degrees of "inadequate regulation" or "institutional oversight."[4]

9. Some experts claim that several major players responsible for creating and distributing mortgage-backed bonds did not sufficiently assess the risk of these collateralized debt obligations (CDOs). Others mention that banks over-loaned to borrowers, since the housing market had been steadily increasing for the fourteen years prior to the collapse[5]...and so on.

10. Of course all of these explanations are correct and evident on some level. However, even the best of these experts has very limited knowledge pertaining to the true causes—and the eventual outcomes—of these events. Nor do they know how to avoid these events. Regarding

this and all important business matters, only one true expert exists.

11. The designer of the entire system (God-Creator) is the single greatest expert. We call this expert the best consultant in the world. This best consultant never gives erroneous or miscalculated guidance. The best consultant always shows you the shortest, easiest ways to acquire more money than you could ever want or need. You need only find its (his or her) "phone number."

12. All miscalculation or error results from inaccurate human judgment. Inaccurate human judgment is evident when clear thought is blocked by imbalanced emotions. Inaccurate judgment is also to be expected when one acts with insufficient forethought or insufficient knowledge.

13. It is well enough to control your emotions; however, even the greatest forethought cannot compensate for a lack of knowledge. And no person has complete knowledge of all that is. Human knowledge is therefore, when regarding the most important circumstances, largely insufficient.

14. Only when guided by the best consultant can you be sure that the knowledge upon which your decisions rest is sufficient.

15. If the best consultant does not guide you, to have earned any amount of money, whether it is billions or

millions of dollars so far, is not to be immune to error in business. Nor does it ensure the long-term security and growth of your current wealth.

16. You are by now becoming familiar with the essential premise that all things are the design of an omni-loving, omnipresent, omniscient, God-Creator. This God-Creator designs all events for your and its constructive benefit.

17. The recent financial crisis or black swan phenomenon is also beneficial. This crisis has already incited new knowledge, growth, and improved methods for managing our individual investments and our global economy. It has prompted us to higher intellectual levels. We have progressed one small step forward. It has forced us to question, think about, and search for its causes. Much still remains to be learned from these events. However, it is clear that the ultimate results of this catalyst are and will be enormously advantageous—both financially and otherwise.

18. This black swan has also brought into focus the emotional panic and fear that can permeate markets—and surface during critical moments in business. This is especially relevant, but not exclusive, to traders, stock brokers, and investment firms. Under no circumstances should you conduct your business or make any decisions under the false guidance of un-mastered or fear-driven emotions.

19. It is fearful panic that has driven some of the greatest and wealthiest business people of our time to act impulsively. The results have been to their and their company's detriment. Panic and fear are reactions to stress. All stress is a direct result of perception. Your perception largely reflects the stage of the evolutionary creation during which you live and your level of personal development.

20. To empower your perception, you must remember that the world is designed by an omni-loving, omni-knowledgeable God-Creator for your and its benefit. The benefits are mutual. The laws are impartial. They serve you and your Creator. When you realize this, stress disappears. All stress is replaced with a strategic search for your and/or your company's most immediate benefits in that situation.

21. It is shown that periods of unfounded euphoria or overconfidence permeates financial markets.[6] Euphoria and overconfidence (arrogance) hinder a person's judgment. These and related states release intense chemicals into the brain and body. The result is a biochemical imbalance that impedes clear judgment. It is obvious that heightened states serve beneficial functions in the design of your life and experiences. They should be balanced if you are to use them for your advantage.

22. Fear is another sensation that permeates trading and investment markets. Fear produces adrenaline, cortisol,

and related hormonal imbalances in your brain that inhibit clear, creative thought. When fear sets in, the ability to develop sophisticated, constructive, beneficial solutions is hindered, if not eliminated entirely.

23. Before making any trade or investment decision, ask yourself what your primary motive is at this moment—the motive beneath the apparent motive. Many find that unbalanced emotions drive their behavior more than they previously knew.

24. When experiencing stress, panic, euphoria, or any other excessive biochemical-psychological state, remember that your perception of any event will dictate your behavior and decision-making. A structured perception that is aligned with omni-knowledge results in superior decisions. Traders and investors, especially, must be cautious of making decisions based on fear, euphoria, and arrogance.

25. Creating new levels of success, happiness, and fulfillment requires expanding your current thought patterns. The only way to expand your current thought patterns is to acquire new knowledge. By acquiring new knowledge, you develop new perspectives, greater insight, and you open your mind to new and higher levels of achievement and success.

26. Investment experts rely heavily on the past to predict the future.[7] Based on this thinking (as much as it may

sound strange), they judge particular events to be "certain" when these events actually *do not* occur 20 percent of the time. They regard other events as "impossible" when they *indeed occur* 20 percent of the time.[8] These misguided judgments are quite common and not unique to investors. These misguided judgments are the result of limited thought patterns.

27. When you access the best consultant in the world, you expand your thought patterns. You are guided by omni-knowledge in addition to explicitly tangible human knowledge. (Some people call it "gut instinct"… but it is more than this.) Success and wealth come faster and in higher quantities…more than ever before. Your alignment with this knowledge provides you with the power that allows you to manage, or react to, all that you encounter with utmost perfection. Stress gradually disappears and is replaced with higher performance, joy, and better results.

28. Only one power has all the information pertinent to your cause. No amount of human research or knowledge is omni-knowledge. Sufficient research and knowledge are required for all things in business to grow. But action and implementation of data-driven knowledge should occur *after* accessing the best consultant.

29. Only the best consultant, God-Creator, as the designer and creator of the system, knows every element

required for your total success. By realizing the design of a pragmatically omni-loving, omni-knowledgeable, omniscient God-Creator, you align yourself with the greatest creative power. This means that you gain access to the best information available. In this way your long-standing rewards are assured.

30. This omni-loving God-Creator wants you to be enormously successful in all that you do. Your desire for success is its desire to act through you—for your and its benefit. Align yourself with this most powerful channel—the source of all power and knowledge. This is how you open yourself to living the life you've always dreamed of living, owning the home(s) you've always wanted, traveling to the places you've always wanted to visit...

31. To do business, trade, or invest without accessing the best consultant is to act based on very limited human knowledge. Doing this may sometimes yield success—but an incomplete formula guarantees only incomplete results.

32. A most complete formula for success relies upon your consistently accessing the omni-knowledge from the best consultant before you conduct important business. This eliminates the likelihood of being ruled by fleeting or misleading emotions. It also aligns you with complete power, omni-knowledge, and creative genius.

33. The more you realize the existence of God-Creator's design, the better you'll do. When you act according to the laws of the design, you progress toward your godlike state—you make fewer mistakes. You make the correct, most beneficial decisions. Even what initially appears to be a "wrong" decision is, in fact, a necessary step closer to the right decisions.

34. When you recognize the coherence of this world, you begin to align yourself with it. Your body and mind produce chemicals that are favorable. These chemicals elicit balance, creative thought, and wealth. You are acting in accordance with your physical design. Consistent action from this foundation assures long-term success. Your decision-making abilities become superior.

35. Consistent access to the best consultant in the world guarantees your success. This is because an omni-knowledgeable God-Creator has more information than you do. This omni-knowledgeable God-Creator will guide you through the intricate components of its creation, toward actions that serve you and your interests. This is already evident by the fact that the information herein has reached you.

36. Limited knowledge limits your perception and vice versa. Because we humans lack explicit omni-knowledge, it may be unclear to us at times of high tension that what seems like a loss is, in fact, a higher gain.

Sometimes the way we want things to work out at a particular moment is not really to our ultimate benefit. By aligning ourselves with the best consultant and knowing that we are guided (even implicitly) by its omni-knowledge, we know that all is working in our favor—even if we cannot yet decode our future winnings from this situation.

37. What we consider a long time is for the creative power mere fractions of seconds. That uniformity of time is an illusion is a precise physical law of the design. Use this law to broaden your awareness. This law alone, when internalized, will increase the scope of your thought patterns. It enables you to think beyond the restrictions and confines of apparent "time." You will begin to notice more opportunities than before. As your thought patterns expand, so do you, so does your influence, and so does your power.

38. Stock market trading, investment, business ventures, and other activities that you undertake are courses that you take in the University of Life toward godlikeness. So do things "right," do your best, enjoy the process, and have fun. Once you realize that all you encounter is part of the grand design and working in your favor, the process is not only more enjoyable, but you act and react to all events in a way that is much more rewarding for you.

39. The world is designed by an omni-loving, omniscient, omnipotent God-Creator. By aligning yourself with this God-Creator via contemplation followed by meditation, you are retraining your mind and empowering the structure of your brain—increasing its level of performance. You're guided to act in accordance with the laws and structure of the design—even those laws that still remain undiscovered. Since all that you encounter is for your and God-Creator's benefit, you need only focus on finding your highest benefits (without taking advantage of others) in all situations to achieve your maximum success.

40. To consistently align with the highest power is to ensure consistent, long-term wealth and fulfillment. This week continue to practice retraining your mind at all times in accordance with the realization that everything occurs for your and God-Creator's benefit. This practice should become internalized, until it is the natural way of the mind. When a person reacts to events based on this recognition, he or she undoubtedly creates new and higher levels of performance, harmony, wealth, happiness, and joy. The returns secured gigantically outweigh the initial investment.

41. In addition to retraining your mind, another exercise is important: Prior to all that you do pertaining to business this week, consult the best consultant. To do this,

silence the senses. Meditate. At the start of meditation, express your gratitude for every event in your life, and then request the wisdom and guidance to make the best possible decisions.

42. When you access God-Creator's power and omni-wisdom, you align your entire being with these forces. You are implicitly guided by all knowledge (seen and unseen) pertinent to your cause. You access divine creativity. You awaken dormant intelligence. You cohesively structure the cells of your brain and body for perfect health and perfect action. You begin to act and react in ways that create the highest levels of success, both known and yet unknown to humankind.

43. To act with enormous wisdom in trades, investment, and business you must first request it. Go and receive your guidance in the silence this week—it awaits you.

44. Soon we will share the single most potent belief that permeates much of our society—one that should be transcended. This sole belief causes many people of even great power to act (unknowingly) against their own interests…But first, accustom yourself to the best consultant's omni-knowledge and the creative power that accompanies it. This will propel you forward enormously.

PART VI

Profit in Global Markets: Leaders' New Patterns of Thinking

You can't be a successful trader, broker, hedge fund manager, investor, or businessperson without understanding the effect that globalization has on all of our lives.

Humanity has made enormous progress since the Stone Age, for example. The world is fast becoming more ideologically unified. We are approaching a state of global agreement.

One can view these changes toward global agreement as mere happenstance, a string of unlawfully guided accidents. It is also possible to recognize that our progress toward global agreement is divinely and lawfully designed—simply a part of evolutionary creation.

One of the greatest teachers of humanity, Jesus Christ, once said, "I tell you that if two of you on earth are in agreement about anything you ask for, it will be done for you by my Father in heaven. For, where two or three come together in my name there am I with them."[1]

Similarly, a state of complete global agreement enables humans to receive all that they desire; it is a state of global godlikeness or "heaven."

Multi-national corporations (MNCs) help to facilitate such global agreement. They are one of the ways by which global ideologies can be reconciled—and mutually accepted by the partnering nations involved. It is therefore essential that MNC leaders (CEOs, minority and majority shareholders) understand the mechanisms of God-Creator's design, thus ensuring the highest benefits for both their companies and the nations in which they operate.

Like in any other situation, where we act in disharmony with God-Creator's design, the results we secure are inevitably lacking. Of course the best Ivy League educations and extended life experience can complement one's knowledge of the design. However, these technical understandings do not replace universal knowledge.

To act without knowledge of the mechanisms and laws that guide God-Creator's design is to yield conflicting and incomplete results. It is to act on insufficient information.

Knowledge of the design—and its laws—is ultimately required when facing the tasks and goals encountered by MNCs, financial and political leaders, and anyone who strives to be the best that he or she can be.

PART VI

1. Multinational Corporations (CEOs and shareholders) play an essential role in the world's socio-economic structure. According to a deterministic perspective, they are vital components and catalysts for change and progress.

2. It is to their advantage to be in the forefront of change. This means acting in accordance with the physical and spiritual laws of God-Creator's system. Doing so yields greater long and short-term benefits for their companies, themselves, and the world at large.

3. As previously noted, Jesus Christ once said, "I tell you that if two of you on earth are in agreement about anything you ask for, it will be done for you by my Father in heaven. For, where two or three come together in my name there am I with them."[2]

4. The state of agreement as mentioned by Jesus Christ can occur when all people have reached a state of full godlikeness. To be godlike is to possess godlike wisdom and knowledge. It is to be powerful, happy, successful, and entirely fulfilled in every way. Becoming more

godlike means making all the money you want and having the harmonious, loving relationships that you desire. Godlikeness within fosters agreement without.

5. The condition of global godlikeness characterizes heaven. The heaven of which Jesus often spoke is a state of global being. For this state to exist in full, both inside and outside of the individual, harmony between all nations is required.

6. Harmony between nations is a reflection of the individuals and leaders in those nations. It is more than an absence of conflict; it is agreement.

7. Globalization (as opposed to separatism or sectarianism) is one of the primary forces leading to the state of agreement noted by Jesus Christ. Where ideas, practices, and technologies are shared, countries come to learn of and respect differing cultures. This breeds acceptance and eventual appreciation of the other. Agreement is inevitable.

8. Globalization is therefore, as are all things, an essential part of evolutionary creation. In evolutionary creation everything is in the process of becoming. When the element of time is removed, it is easier to see that the entirety of our human journey toward godlikeness is essentially "instantaneous."

9. MNCs (like Microsoft, for instance) play a key role in the globalizing aspect of evolutionary creation. Entering new markets requires bridging cultural gaps. MNCs, by the essence of their activity, help to bridge these gaps and elicit acceptance between cultures. Where cultures understand, respect, and rely upon each other, we have global agreement rather than global conflict.

10. Mutual acceptance and understanding between cultures is a basic component of MNC success. The simple acts of penetrating and maintaining markets, recruiting, interacting with and retaining foreign staff members expands cultural awareness for all individuals within MNCs—both expats and locals.

11. MNCs are forced to customize and market products in ways that appeal to what we call "foreign" markets. Sales practices have to be adapted to suit local needs. Expats and country locals must work cooperatively toward common goals. An understanding of the "other" decreases cultural conflict. It is shown that countries that understand or accept each other's ideologies are less likely to engage in conflict or war.[3]

12. Commonly held generalizations that often cause global conflict soon vanish in MNC settings. Take, for example, major economic powers, such as the United States, Japan, Canada, and certain European markets.

These amenable relations exemplify the beginnings of more advanced globalization.

13. Although they have received much criticism, MNCs exist, as do all things, by design. The less-developed countries they enter advance in many ways. MNC presence is more beneficial than not for all involved; however, challenges to minimize negative impacts remain.

14. A primary motive of a MNC is to generate profits for shareholders (which is legitimate from a design perspective). However, there has been a tendency (intentionally and unintentionally) to accomplish this at the expense of social responsibility. Critics often say that MNCs create many problems in the countries they enter. Such problems can include pollution, resource depletion, economic over-dependence, and unfairly low wages, among others.

15. To discuss social issues: It is a basic law of God-Creator's design that one should not take advantage of another person or entity. Doing so reduces ultimate profit and eventually leads to equivalent loss. While immediate profit may be gained by taking advantage of another, this action conflicts with God-Creator's basic design and, therefore, a company's long-term interests. Where action appears to conflict with the laws and design of the universe, creative solutions are required.

16. Obviously MNC CEOs are aware that much is to be gained by adequately addressing environmental, social, and a foreign country's local cultural needs. Doing so generates wider consumer support, which generates profit and shareholder support.

17. However, sometimes an inherent conflict may arise between generating substantial profit and addressing social, cultural, or environmental issues. Mutually profitable solutions are essential.

18. The best solutions are always creative (of what we call divine inspiration). They coincide with the laws of God-Creator's design. When you act in accordance with God-Creator's structure, you align yourself with the most powerful, benevolent, and creative forces in the universe. Your enduring achievement is assured.

19. The more you act in accordance with God-Creator's design, the more easily attained and more enduring is your financial success. Knowledge of the laws of God-Creator's design is therefore of incalculable value. The degree to which your thoughts and actions are aligned with God-Creator's design determines your success, fulfillment, and happiness in every area of life. This is the key to having the power and freedom to travel at whim, to develop your perfect career, to be able to buy and be anything that you want at any moment.

20. When you act in synchronization with God-Creator's omniscience and omnipotence, you make better decisions and form much more creative solutions. Harmonizing your thoughts and actions with God-Creator's design is like accessing the best consultant (discussed earlier).

21. Under the best consultant's guidance, basic functions, such as marketing, recruiting, and retaining the best local management team or managing strategic and investment decisions, are accomplished more effectively (and elicit higher reward values) than before. This is because you are guided by God-Creator's omniscience, as opposed to being exclusively guided by inherently limited human knowledge. It is impossible to make "mistakes" with the best consultant's guidance.

22. The best consultant enables you to even better respond to the quickly changing priorities of the global business landscape. You anticipate potential developments and hurdles before they arise. You resolve apparent conflicts between social responsibility and raising profits with an ease never before experienced.

23. The best consultant has omniscience (knowledge of all that is). Knowledge is the most versatile and therefore most valuable commodity. This is even truer when considering the laws upon which this universe functions. When you know, and can therefore act in accordance with the laws of God-Creator's design, your performance

increases on every level. *A Guide to Your Supreme Power* provides knowledge of these laws. The impact of this knowledge is positive, beneficial, and rewarding everywhere in your life.

24. One of the most important aspects of God-Creator's physical, psychological, and neurological design is the human body. An understanding of your brain and body allows you to better control and maximize their functions to your benefit. This increases the quality of your performance in all areas.

25. The brain is a primary aspect of the human design. It is the seat of all experience and decision. Your brain and mind determine your perception (see Part III for further discussion). Your perception determines the interpretation and quality of every life experience. It also frames the decision-making process.

26. Your mind's thought patterns and your brain's corresponding chemical processes guide all perception (and decision-making). Your thought patterns and chemical processes serve your highest benefits when you recognize that all is the direct result of the design of a pragmatically omni-loving, omniscient, omnipotent God-Creator.

27. When you interpret every event as the result of an omni-loving God-Creator for your and its benefit, you perceive each situation in the most advantageous way. This recognition

alone increases the quality of all related decisions. Maintaining this perception is just part of the required equation.

28. The human brain is unable to absorb every bit of information with which it is presented. It therefore only retrieves information that matters to a person. Information matters to the extent that it ignites emotion circuits in the brain.[4] The emotion circuits that promote information absorption can range anywhere from mild curiosity to elation or anxiety.[5]

29. All accumulated knowledge in the brain is therefore connected—either directly or indirectly—to emotion. In this manner our emotions influence even our most mundane decisions. Economists once believed that decisions could be made rationally on cost-benefit analysis alone,[6] but frontier neuroscience shows us otherwise.

30. What we once thought took place only in the prefrontal cortex (the linguistic and math reasoning portion of the brain) extends to the limbic system (the emotion center of the brain). At the mere hint of a distant reward or benefit, your brain releases the neurotransmitter dopamine, which alters thought patterns and influences decision-making.[7]

31. Even more, it has been shown that when presented with an excessively low offer in negotiations, even the most educated and successful people exhibit unfavorable

emotional reactions. They thereafter reject offers that would result in considerable financial gain. The subsequent offers are rejected to subconsciously punish the other party for the initially upsetting offer.[8] This and similar behavioral patterns occur because the initial release of epinephrine and similar biochemicals have not yet abated. In this way the release of emotional chemicals influences decision-making in what we call real time.

32. One way to change the destructive nature of potentially negative, emotion-induced decision-making is to generate balanced, constructive emotions. This can be done by following the principle, "Love your enemy (or adversary or partner) as yourself." When you train your mind to view all interpersonal encounters from this perspective, you find that even the subtlest emotional upsets cease to occur.

33. To be able to love or have no negative feelings toward another requires that you first love yourself. Upon consistently recognizing that you are a perfect creation of an omnipotent, omni-loving God-Creator and that you are created in its image and likeness, you naturally accept and love yourself. This is not a naïve, narcissistic, or selfish act. It is simply the awareness that you (like everyone else) have a divine purpose and right to exist on your journey toward godlikeness.

34. This recognition also prevents you from behaving aggressively, since aggression is simply a manifestation of

fear—the need to protect yourself or your ego from perceived threat. When you know your inherent godlikeness, these ego-induced behavioral tendencies are replaced by more constructive thought patterns—thoughts of higher integrity, wisdom, and knowledge. These thought patterns allow your mind to more easily access the brain's knowledge.

35. As history and our most current political, financial, and economic events teach us, even the most intelligent humans working together do not have knowledge of *all* that pertains to their desired goals. Of course professional human knowledge is essential for any serious endeavor; however, even the best Ivy League education and extended experience is insufficient on its own in the face of tasks and goals that MNCs or financial and political leaders might encounter daily.

36. Here is just one "small" example where nearly infinite can be found: When American companies initially entered China, they acted on the assumption that China had trade secret laws equivalent to those in the United States. Consequently, these American companies shared various trade secrets with key natives and were soon competing against their own technologies in the same markets.

37. Access to omniscience not only prevents such events but also aligns your decisions with the divine design.

Of course potentially negative experiences elicit growth, knowledge, and development—but it is to your advantage to make all things contribute to your end, as much as possible, in the most pleasant (not painful) way.

38. To access the omniscience required for perfect business expansion, you should access the best consultant.

39. In accessing the best consultant you integrate and process all the knowledge that you have acquired thus far in your life. This integration can include knowledge from both the academic world and life experience. It also provides you with omniscience. You make fewer decisional mistakes. Apparently conflicting interests are resolved. Success in every endeavor is assured.

40. The way to be sure that all actions contribute to both your long- and short-term gains is to access the best consultant. The way to integrate all knowledge pertinent to your cause is to access the best consultant—in the silence. To help prevent adverse emotional influences and to extend the scope of your knowledge in decision-making…access the best consultant.

41. It is best to solve conflicting interests via accessing the best consultant in the silence. Research shows that meditative silence increases creative genius.[9] Those who consistently access this have enormous advantage over others. They respond creatively to challenges.

They exhibit a rare poise that develops only when a person knows that all things occur by the design of an omni-loving, omniscient, omnipotent, God-Creator and that all things function in perfect coherence according to basic universal laws.

42. Your greatest achievements will surface when you consistently utilize the power of the design to assist your causes—rather than acting, as most do, unknowingly against these great creative forces. Acting against these great forces creates disharmony. Disharmony inevitably causes delays, and delays are evidenced by profit loss and missed opportunities.

43. This week search for any areas in your life and business where you think you might be unintentionally (or intentionally) responsible for another being, group, country, or entity being taken unfair advantage of. If you happen to find such an area in life and/or business, go into the silence. Access the best consultant. Request a creative solution. Request the exact guidance to effectively implement this creative solution in a way that benefits all involved and beyond.

44. The solution may not arrive instantaneously, since it typically does not. But do this exercise each day this week and wait for the answer to creatively "occur" to you. When it does, simply follow through as you usually would.

45. You will find this to be a most effective strategy for all apparent challenges or conflicts in business and life. Use it whenever needed. This method, when consistently exercised as you see fit, will ensure your enduring success via right decision and right action. It is the perfect tool for those who desire to come as close as possible to all godlike characteristics in this life-time and now.

46. Knowing the laws upon which the universe is built is an enormous advantage; accepting as truth those that do not influence real outcomes can only misinform our efforts. This will be clarified in full in the upcoming chapters. For now, become familiar with the strategy as outlined above. Learn that it works, so you may overcome all present and future challenges in such a way that your solutions harmonize with God-Creator's perfect design. When they do you activate enormous creative power in favor of your interests.

PART VII

Eliminate Failure Forever: Transcend the Two Most Limiting Beliefs

When we act from the basis of inaccurate (or simply outdated) information we are significantly weakened, which makes it almost impossible to secure what we want in life. The more that we're acquainted with truth, the more empowered we are, the more money we can make, the more harmonious are our relationships, and the more successful we can be.

But, many mistaken "truths" permeate our belief system. These ideas are often endorsed by society, which includes, of course, science and religion. It's important to remember that science and religion merely reflect the current stages of humanity. As we humans develop, so do science and religion. Consequently, both science and religion have historically believed and advocated inaccurate truths.

The "illusion of truth" phenomenon shows that when people are repeatedly exposed to a concept or idea they simply accept it as true. This acceptance is based on a mental familiarity that occurs when we are not explicitly aware of having been exposed to a given idea.[1] The process is therefore subconscious.

We are least aware of repeatedly endorsed ideas when they simply permeate our paradigm (our collective belief system). For example, people once believed that the sun circled the earth. They also believed that the earth was flat. People once believed that all matter was solid.

These ideas were thought to be true, but they were hardly ever consciously considered. Many ideas of the same category exist today. Given their inherently deceptive nature, these unquestioned ideas can only mislead and weaken the efforts that stem from them.

This chapter discusses some of the deeply permeated (yet now shown to be false) ideas upon which our collective thoughts rest. One such idea is the acceptance of "original sin" as proposed over two thousand years ago.

By correcting these and other false thought foundations, we correct all that is constructed upon them. Gigantic power is acquired as a result...the power to create the life of your dreams, to earn the income you've always wanted, to openly engage in loving, harmonious relationships, and more…

PART VII

1. Every person functions in accordance with at least two basic systems of beliefs. One belief system is the system of which we are consciously aware. The other belief system functions below the level of awareness. This is the one that (in accordance with your ego) structures your interpretation of the world. It is called your "paradigm."

2. All incoming stimuli—your perceptions—are filtered through your paradigm, which contains the beliefs that you have about yourself and reality. Your paradigm determines how you relate to and interact with the world.[2]

3. The societies in which we live strongly influence our individual paradigms. For example, once people believed that the earth was flat. Most individuals took this belief for granted; they did not explicitly question it. According to this and other seemingly true and unquestioned beliefs endorsed by society (including science and religion), people interpreted the world around them. Any interpretations that were based on the assumption that the earth was flat were inaccurate.

4. Such inaccurate beliefs cause people to incorrectly interpret the world around them—and therefore to ineffectively respond to its events. Inaccurate beliefs limit your ability to recognize God-Creator's design; they do not serve your highest interests.

5. The more that the beliefs of your paradigm are accurate and coincide with the laws upon which the universe operates, the more you function in accordance with God-Creator's design—the more your energy is constructively and coherently channeled toward your goals, aspirations, and happiness. And only when your energy is *constructively* channeled toward your goals and aspirations will you begin making the amount of money that constitutes complete financial freedom and joy for you.

6. All happiness, creative power, and success are contingent on being in harmony with God-Creator's perfect design. For this reason it is imperative that the beliefs in your paradigm are fundamentally and technically accurate. Where technical accuracy cannot be ensured, a consistent recognition of God-Creator's pragmatically omni-loving, omnipotent, omniscient, and omnipresent nature is essential.

7. As in societies throughout history, several outdated and, so, inaccurate beliefs prevail in our society's current paradigm. Unless you have consciously examined

and corrected them, they permeate your individual thought processes. This means that it is highly likely that outdated and inaccurate assumptions are currently determining how you interpret and respond to the ever-changing world. This influences your income, your relationships, and your social life.

8. Potentially inaccurate assumptions and beliefs can determine where you find yourself, intellectually, financially, and emotionally, five to ten years from now… or even tomorrow. Inaccurate beliefs cannot bring you closer to understanding the design and therefore do not serve your interests.

9. Of the numerous known and unknown incorrect assumptions that permeate our society's paradigm, one such assumption is the concept of uniform time. Time does not have an absolute existence outside of your thought processes. While the concept of time makes change and order more comprehensible for us, it is not a physical, universal law, as humans once believed.[3]

10. The sensory or perceptual illusion of uniform time encourages people to think in a strictly linear manner. This constricted tendency limits a person's thought patterns and creative ability.

11. As Jesus, one of the greatest teachers, told his disciples, "Have you discovered the beginning, that you are

seeking the end?" Similarly, the sensory illusion of time can falsely lead us to think in terms of beginnings and ends. It limits our scope of reality.

12. This linear understanding of course helps people function in our clock-driven world. However, it is important to remember that uniform time does not fundamentally exist. Viewing the world and its events in accordance to purely linear thought mechanisms is inconsistent with the true nature of God-Creator's design. For God-Creator, time does not fundamentally exist; it is not part of the physical design of the universe. It is not a law upon which to interpret reality, as previously believed.

13. Jesus knew that the source of creation transcends linear thought patterns. When you realize that time does not exist at the level of creation—that it is not an absolute aspect of the design—the accuracy of your paradigm is strengthened. You do not falsely interpret or attempt to decipher your world in accordance with this inaccurate assumption.

14. By recognizing that uniform time is a sensory illusion—simply an outdated and incomplete belief that currently permeates the collective paradigm—your thought patterns expand. Your possibilities increase, as do your influence and total success. Change is viewed differently. Learning that the earth was round (and that it orbits around the sun—not vice versa) increased human

possibility. The same will occur with the understanding that uniform time is, at the most fundamental level of design, nonexistent. Transcending our mental (and physical-mathematical) reliance on time may be central to furthering human space travel abilities.

15. Time as a concept or idea makes change and order in the world easier for us to comprehend. It is a necessary function of human perception at this and previous stages of our evolutionary creation. It is a direct result of our physical design (our senses) endowed by an omni-loving God-Creator to serve rather than constrain us. Once we know that uniform time does not fundamentally exist, we no longer feel pressured or confined by its apparent limits on a daily basis.

16. Time does not physically exist. It is believed that a unified theory of physics would require the elimination of the concept entirely. This knowledge will become further widespread and more common as evolutionary creation (the human journey toward godlikeness) progresses.

17. Inherent in evolutionary creation is the casting aside of obsolete ideas when we are presented with new information. Indeed, the fact that you are presented with a piece of information regarding the design means that you are intellectually and spiritually ready for it. This is because new information is accompanied by an expansion of personal influence, which requires an equivalent

degree of what we call, for communicative purposes, "spiritual" responsibility. By design, with information and knowledge comes increased power and, therefore, greater accountability. Where the spiritual does not mature to accommodate expanded power, influence is brief.

18. Sometimes key information regarding the design is presented in the form of a divine myth. There are widely accepted mythical interpretations that once served humans in their state of evolutionary creation, but which are now outdated. Once a myth, or its interpretation, is outdated, it no longer serves its proper function in the design.

19. Churches, synagogues, temples, and mosques are depositories of the divine truths contained in biblical and other scriptural myths. More than three thousand years ago, biblical myths were delivered according to human intellectual abilities of that time. Just as you would not explain the nature of chemistry or physics to a very young child or to an ancestor of the Stone Age, the nature and structure of our universe could not be directly explained to people—they simply would not have understood.

20. Frontier science continuously demonstrates the ordered complexity, upon which our universe rests. Had this been explicitly outlined in biblical form three

thousand years ago, the entire book would have been dismissed as readily as many seemingly outlandish futurist ideas are dismissed today.

21. For the Bible to maintain value throughout "time," it was written in multiple dimensions.[4] This multi-dimensional structure enables humans to decode its different dimensions, according to their particular intellectual, technological, and spiritual stage at any given point. As evolutionary creation progresses, so do human tools and intellect. Humans can thus de-code more and more of the meaning behind the Bible and its myths.

22. While we have so far begun to expose four dimensions of the Bible, there are likely even more dimensions. Even as a four-dimensional account, the Bible has been shown to both predict the future and confirm the past.[5] As our scientific and intellectual abilities to decipher more dimensions of the Bible increase, so will our knowledge of God-Creator's design.

23. Even the simple one-dimensional myths in the Bible directly pertain to and can reveal aspects of God-Creator's design. These myths are meant to be interpreted and reinterpreted, according to our stage of evolutionary creation.

24. A myth's interpretations have value to the extent that they beneficially serve humanity. With the progres-

sion of humanity toward godlikeness comes an advanced interpretation of its myths. Since all interpretations are subject to the limits of human reason at any time, it is everyone's duty to cast aside those that no longer coincide with our expanded intellectual abilities.

25. A long-standing interpretation of the Adam and Eve myth still permeates our society's paradigm. This special relic once benefited humanity enormously. It enabled people to interpret and understand the world in accordance with their intellect and growth. It helped them explain their perceived suffering—after all, according to this interpretation, everyone was expelled from paradise.

26. Humanity has since developed (intellectually, scientifically, etc.). We are in a more advanced stage of evolutionary creation (the human journey toward godlikeness). Now, this once beneficial interpretation contains outdated beliefs that form the obvious basis from which a person may act against his or her own best interests.

27. This mythical interpretation is so strongly woven into our collective paradigm that it influences the psychological thought processes of those who do not consider themselves religious at all.

28. More than two thousand years ago, a revered theologian named Augustine of Hippo interpreted the meaning of the story of Adam and Eve.[6] He determined

that Eve was tricked into eating a fruit from the Tree of Knowledge...and that this act had been previously forbidden by God-Creator.

29. Upon consuming this fruit, Eve and Adam lost their innocence. They were exiled from Paradise. They were cursed with having a sinful nature. All humans were subsequently cursed with an inherently sinful nature as well. They deserved and lived in a state of punishment. They were unworthy of Paradise and had to live their lives in repentance.

30. Augustine's interpretation of this myth elicited his theory of primordial sin. This theory was a blessing for humanity at the start of the fourth century. It corresponded with the limits of human reason and intellectual or scientific understandings at that time. It was an essential component during earlier phases of evolutionary creation.

31. Humanity has since progressed enormously. Now, over two thousand years later, Augustine's interpretation no longer coincides with our state of evolutionary creation. The time has come for more advanced insight.

32. A reevaluation of the myth has long been required. According to this biblical story of Adam and Eve, God created humans in God's image and likeness. This means Adam (or human) must be godlike and perfect. A perfect God-Creator can only create a perfect creature.

33. Augustine's interpretation of the Adam and Eve myth, while once valuable, now contains logical fallacies that no longer hold merit for the contemporary reader.

34. Adam and Eve were created by a perfect creator, which means that both of them were perfect as well—perfect for God-Creator's purposes and therefore their own. Perfectly created entities (as the concept of "perfect" implies) cannot disobey God-Creator's will. A perfect entity would simply never disobey its creator.

35. It is also impossible to disobey a God-Creator that is omnipotent. Where God-Creator is omnipotent, deviance is impossible, because deviance requires a degree of power on behalf of the deviant. It is important to recall that all power is of the same source and quality. Where a person is not synchronized with the power of God-Creator, he or she may have only fleetingly apparent power but not actual power.

36. Adam and Eve were thus not only too perfect to disobey God-Creator, but an omnipotent God-Creator has all power. This leaves humans no power for disobedience. If the event was part of God-Creator's grand design (as all are), it cannot be deemed an act of disobedience. Indeed, it was intentionally designed to happen by God-Creator for both creation and humanity's benefit.

37. To further analyze this multi-dimensional myth, if God-Creator is omnipotent, this means that the

serpent that coaxed Eve to eat the "forbidden fruit" did so entirely by God-Creator's will. This confrontation, as are all, was designed for God-Creator's and humanity's benefit.

38. If an omnipotent God-Creator designed the event in which Eve ate the fruit from the Tree of Knowledge, this means that God-Creator *wanted* Eve to eat this fruit (or at least created the myth of her doing so). The myth's message suggests that only by eating from the Tree of Knowledge could humans enter the journey and process toward godlikeness. The Tree of Knowledge is a metaphor for science and experience—both of which uncover key aspects of the design.

39. To become godlike one must understand and act in accordance with God-Creator's design. This means human experience and knowledge of science is required. The Tree of Knowledge or scientific progress in synergy with The Tree of Life (spiritual growth) is required for our evolutionary creation toward godlikeness.

40. To become godlike, a person must act in accordance with both the material and spiritual laws of God-Creator's design. The spiritual laws are metaphorically represented in this myth by the Tree of Life. God-Creator's design thus contains a precise combination of spiritual and physical laws. Only when you are intellectually and, so to speak, spiritually ready, is scientific information

pertaining to the design delivered. (This can be better understood when considering humans and nuclear power; it is in God-Creator's interest that the act of creation reaches completion).

41. Both science and spirituality progress in unison, helping humans advance toward godlikeness, by design. Once considered two contrasting ideas, today they are complimentary approaches toward the same progression. The once beneficial notion that these two methods of knowing inherently conflict has long since become antiquated.

42. Augustine's theory of original sin has permeated our paradigm since the fourth century. It has become an outdated assumption that causes individuals to feel guilty or devalue themselves and to act against themselves unknowingly—it influences people's self-esteem, thinking, and behavior at the level below conscious awareness. It has this effect until it is brought to conscious awareness, evaluated, and, if necessary, replaced with more constructive beliefs.

43. Humans were designed by an omni-loving, omnipotent God-Creator. It is important to remember that God-Creator's act of creation still continues. It was only the illusion of time that led Augustine to think that creation had already occurred and that humans were now living in a state of ruin or downfall—a state of sin. What appears to be thousands of years for a human is

mere fractions of a second for an all-powerful, eternal God-Creator. The act of creation is still in progress; this is the essence of the term evolutionary creation.

44. By realizing and recognizing God-Creator's omnipower and perfection, you align yourself with this creative force. Your success and advancement in all things is assured. In this way you get all the things you've always wanted…the cars, the homes, the vacations, the career, the money, the loving relationships, and more.

45. This week, go into the silence as before. For it is during contemplation, followed by meditation, that deep-seated beliefs in your paradigm surface. It is here that the most potent changes in fundamental perception are made… changes that distinguish "ordinary" people from those of advanced creativity, influence, power, money, and success.

46. During the silence this week, you should proclaim, once and for all, that you are an absolutely perfect human creation of power. You have not inherited some sort of lowly imperfection or sinful nature. These mythical interpretations were stories for small "children" elicited during an earlier period of our evolutionary creation. Such stories no longer serve the scope of our ever-expanding purposes.

47. That you are a perfectly evolving creation in a perfectly coherent design is certain. As you assert this

during initial contemplation, followed by meditation, you are retraining your mind and therefore empowering your brain and body—your physical design—in accordance with these constructive, accurate beliefs. As you strengthen your paradigm, you align yourself with some of the most powerful forces of the universe. You are accessing the ground of creation, the realm where creative genius awaits your fruition.

48. When you consistently align with God-Creator's perfection, you retrain your mind to realize that you are a perfect human rather than a "fallen creature." As this knowledge sets in, you'll notice subtle yet profound changes in your thoughts and behavior. The results of your actions will be unusually beneficial because you are no longer influenced by a simple yet potent theory more suited for archaic times. You are no longer held back by the outdated assumption that humans are inherently imperfect. You relinquish the germ of deep-seated guilt. Your paradigm is strengthened; you do not act unknowingly against your own interests.

49. As you enter the silence this week, replace the entrenched belief in original or primordial sin with an assertion that is in harmony with your level of evolutionary growth, integrity, and understanding: that all things are the perfect design of an omnipotent God-Creator for your and its benefit. You are a creature of perfect creation. You are therefore inherently perfect as well.

As the Bible states, "God created man in its own image and likeness."

50. Keep in mind that uniform time is a sensory illusion, designed to serve your daily affairs rather than constrain your perceptions. This simple understanding will greatly enhance your perspective. It expands your thought patterns, preparing you for further growth, knowledge, and expanded influence. With this expanded influence comes what we call spiritual responsibility. Only when you know and realize your own perfection will you be in a position to recognize the perfection of others; such understandings give rise to effortless creativity and spiritual responsiveness.

51. The ability to constantly see perfection in design, where the average person may not, is essential for growth and fulfillment. To be a leader is to think ahead—to think creatively and constructively—to think differently. You must come to realize your inherent perfection… because you must know something within yourself before you can recognize it anywhere else.

PART VIII

Unleash Your Winning Streak: Mastering Adversarial Situations

In a world designed by an omnipotent, pragmatically omni-loving God-Creator, all perspectives and feelings are legitimate and ultimately serve beneficial functions. Since all situations and people are catalysts for growth in our evolutionary journey toward godlikeness, where we see an enemy in the other, we do ourselves a disservice.

By perceiving another person or group as an evil threat, we directly hinder our ability to fruitfully act. The term "evil" is simply a mental construct, derived from intense negative emotion (such as fear) that clouds constructive thought. Any decisive actions taken during such mental states are largely ineffective.

In fact, it's shown that when people try to resolve conflict based on the fear that another person or group is a threat, the decisions they implement actually perpetuate conflict rather than resolve it.[1] The stronger the fear, the more unconstructive is the person's thinking—as are the solutions that he or she implements.[2]

While we should avoid making strategic decisions during fear-ridden states, there are obvious circumstances in which fear and perceived threat enable us to save and protect our own lives and the lives of others. Feelings of fear and threat therefore serve a definite purpose for survival. They drive us to react during adversarial or even dangerous circumstances.

Even in the face of adversity, challenge, or threat, the concept "Love your enemy as yourself" should guide a person. This concept enables us to transcend the reflexive-thinking styles that perpetuate, rather than resolve, conflict.

Part VIII explains the underlying mechanisms behind this spiritual law. It reveals the most effective and rewarding ways to overcome potential adversaries in any circumstance, both globally and interpersonally.

History shows us that yesterday's enemies are today's friends and vice versa. Humans are social creatures who require the support of others to advance. Thus, the ability to genuinely resolve conflict contains enormous power, because even among the better minds, this ability is still largely uncultivated.

And now, to advance your creative power…Part VIII.

PART VIII

1. Perception is not objective; it is therefore a creative act.[3] As you perceive, so you respond and so you *create* your life. Where perceptions are positive, you develop; where they are negative, you regress. Only by perceiving divine perfection within can you perceive it without. Your greatest gains are realized when you act from the knowledge that all is designed by an omnipotent, omni-loving God-Creator. This is how you come to respond to life in ways that help you earn more money, have loving relationships (rather than enmity), and enjoy all the other pleasures that come with these things…

2. The entire universe functions under laws of perfect order and harmony. Everything is a result of this perfect order—all occurrences and people. Absolutely nothing is arbitrary. All events are vital to evolutionary creation, which is the process of human progress toward godlikeness.

3. Each occurrence and each person serves an especially important function in God-Creator's design, or they simply would not exist. One person's supposed enemy

is another person's love and vice versa. Thus, the concept of enemy has no universal validity. It is a subjective, relative, emotion-laden term. As history shows, yesterday's enemies are today's friends and vice versa.

4. Words such as "evil" or "enemy" represent ideas and serve a specific function in God-Creator's design. For example, they motivate us toward or away from things. They guide our behavior. In a world designed by an omni-loving, omnipotent God-Creator, no laws support evil, nor is there an absence of ultimate good.

5. We associate the idea of "enemy" with pain or evil. It is a result of our inability to understand all aspects of God-Creator's design. What we call painful experiences are catalysts for growth and enhanced awareness. They are prompts to expand our understanding of the design and gain more creative benevolence. In this way we become more godlike. Without these catalysts we would experience no growth and progression toward godlikeness.

6. The word "enemy" describes a force or entity that elicits a sense of threat or potential pain. Fear is the origin of this construct. If you are not afraid of someone or do not view him or her as a threat to your existence, you could not perceive this person as an enemy. However, there are times when it is entirely legitimate to perceive another person, group, or situation as a potential threat.

By practicing the system in *A Guide to Your Supreme Power*, you can better discern genuine threat from that which is nothing more than the fabrication of an over-reactive (egocentric) mind. Indeed, it is excessive fear that reduces even the greatest minds to embrace an outlook of cynicism.

7. In a world designed by an omni-loving God-Creator, all events and circumstances are designed to serve your highest benefits and development. This includes potentially threatening people and situations. Where we perceive legitimate threat, we find a catalyst for action and growth. By thinking constructively and creatively, a person develops the best solutions for all potentially threatening situations. And each person inevitably encounters what we call threatening or challenging situations in life.

8. It is important to constructively respond to threat or danger—but we should be careful not to erroneously perceive threat or an enemy where none really exists. When you think in accordance with the perspectives outlined in *A Guide to Your Supreme Power*, you accurately discern real danger or threat from that which is falsely perceived as threatening but, in fact, is not, (see also the meditation section at the end of *A Guide to Your Supreme Power*).

9. It is known that the more one perceives other people or situations as somehow threatening, the more anxious or uneasy the person generally becomes[4]—the excessive

biochemical effects of which are often unnecessary and unconstructive.

10. In a universe created by an omni-loving God-Creator, we have no need to view another person as a threat or source of fear. When you recognize that all things occur for God-Creator's and everyone's highest mutual benefit, ideas of evil and enemy are eliminated. Challenges are recognized and overcome in the most constructive and beneficial ways. Where we once perceived an evil enemy, we begin to see a catalyst for our own (and others') higher growth and development.

11. Since everyone that you encounter is introduced into your life by an omni-loving God-Creator to serve your, God's, (and their) highest, most noble interests, emotionally viewing people as enemies has no inherent validity. Seeing other people as enemies reduces your ability to fruitfully channel your energy toward getting the things you desire…the car, the lover, the home, the career, the money, the life of your dreams.

12. To proclaim enmity with another in your mind is to do yourself a personal and practical disservice. The Old Testament states, "Love your neighbor as yourself." The amazing teacher, Jesus Christ, took it one step further and, in essence, told his followers to love their enemies as themselves. This teaching was not naïve. He was sharing

a practical insight; indeed, he was sharing a law of God-Creator's design.

13. "Love your enemy as yourself" is a view that should help to guide your perception. This view enables you to think constructively during potentially adversarial circumstances—without getting lost in emotionally ineffective fear and enemy-laden thoughts. It is not a substitute for properly safeguarding yourself but rather a means to more constructively directing your energy. When you love your enemy as yourself you elicit creatively constructive solutions rather than contending with potentially unconstructive thought.

14. For example, each of your thoughts influences your biochemical processes and nervous system. What we call negative, fearful, or angry enemy-centered thoughts produce correspondingly obstructive chemicals into your brain and body. They weaken your nervous system. Fearful, angry thoughts damage cell structures, cloud mental clarity, and discourage power and perfect health, (see PART IV for further discussion).

15. Enemy-centered anger, fear, and stress inhibit clear communication between neurons (cells) in your brain. They directly hinder the ability to form creative solutions during challenging situations. An excessive amount of potentially unsupportive neuropeptides (protein-like molecules) are released into the brain instead.[5]

16. When you understand God-Creator's design, you find that what we call challenging situations become glorious moments of opportunity. There is no enemy. No need for revenge. When you act in unison with God-Creator's design, supportive neuropeptides are released into your brain. Creative thought is fostered. You act and react to your highest advantage. Primitive thought is replaced with creative achievement.

17. Since all people are the creation of an omni-loving, omnipotent God-Creator (in God's image and likeness), all people serve a divine function. To declare otherwise is to view the world and its events chaotically and devoid of the potential for growth. Special people and lucrative opportunities emerge (seemingly magically) in all occurrences; you need only expand your perspectives to recognize them.

18. Anytime you perceive someone as an enemy or friend, you respond accordingly. Each action elicits a like and equal reaction. This is a long-known law upon which the universe functions. Use it for your advantage....Just as negative thoughts adversely affect the brain, body cells, and behavior, any action based on the belief that a person or group is your enemy does not serve you.

19. When you recognize a perceived enemy as a person who is simply in your life for your own advancement, your perspective expands; your focus changes. Analysis is more

creative and solution-driven, and you get better results. New opportunities regarding the situation are presented. You act from a high place of knowledge and creative power. Things are resolved in your favor. Your actions prompt a beneficial sequence of events—both long- and short-term.

20. Humans are social creatures. We cannot advance solely via our own devices. It is better to have forces eager to see your desired end rather than forces eager to see your apparent demise.

21. Creative leaders do not advance by maintaining a fierce collection of enemies or by maintaining superficially false friends. They advance by fully recognizing the value of others and acting in accordance with this basic knowledge of God-Creator's design.

22. Perceiving another person as your enemy or treating another person in an arrogant manner immediately releases a flood of damaging chemicals into your physical body. Actions based on these perceptions elicit corresponding results from the external world. All actions, if they are to serve your interests, must be in harmony with God-Creator's design. This means you must love your enemy as yourself, (for your own sake if for nothing else).

23. To love your enemy as yourself is not to martyr yourself or act against your own interests in any way.

It is simply to discern that each person and event is purposely created by an omnipotent, omniscient, omniloving God-Creator. Each person and event therefore serves a unique and special function in God-Creator's design—or that person or event would not exist. To this end you cannot mistreat or take advantage of others for your assumed benefit. As you assist others in their higher developments, they assist you in yours.

24. All of God-Creator's design—its people, events, and social and business structures—work in perfect order. No person, occurrence or social or business structure is devoid of purpose; everything is perfectly intended. Just as science discovers aspects of God-Creator's design at the proper moment of evolutionary creation, key ancient knowledge is preserved until the proper moment.

25. As a result, the primary teachings of the Bible and Jesus were preserved in the soil for nearly two thousand years. The Christian Church and other religious institutions were designed to play a unique role in preserving these teachings. Thus, religious institutions are historically shown to be intentional (and unintentional) depositories of truth.

26. One such historical example is The First Council of Nicea, which convened in the year AD 325. Many think that it was here that Christian bishops of the time decided which books were and were not going to be part of the

official Christian Bible; however, that is not the case.[6] Athanasius, the Bishop of Alexandria, listed the New Testament canon books in his AD 367 Festal Letter.[7]

27. As a matter of course, many authentic and valuable teachings from Jesus were deemed heretical or unofficial during this time. Anything that was feared as a potential threat to the Church's influence or power was not included in the official canon.

28. The teachings that spoke of or promoted direct knowledge of God were seen as an explicit threat to the Church's influence at that time. The Church saw no political advantage in promoting direct access to God during the first few centuries following Jesus's death. This was likely the reason that any books containing such access were deemed unofficial, and their study, if uncritical, was strictly forbidden.

29. Although the study of these scriptures was prohibited, the scriptures themselves were not always destroyed as the Church requested. One such instance occurred after the First Council of Nicea when Bishop Athanasius condemned the use of all non-canonical Christian books in his Festal Letter of AD 367.[8] Instead of discarding all of its scriptures, the Pachomian monastery buried those that were too valuable to be permanently destroyed.[9] These events, like all others, should be seen as having occurred by design.

30. Indeed, these buried scriptures were not found until 1945. A peasant in Nag Hammadi, Egypt, found (recovered) them. They are now deemed part of the Nag Hammadi library.[10]

31. The Gospel of Thomas is part of the Nag Hammadi library.[11] Containing nothing other than sayings, quotes, and parables of Jesus, this gospel gives everyone equal and direct access to his wisdom. It was fitting that these scriptures were inaccessible until the year 1945. For it is only now that humans have begun to evolve enough—in their process of evolutionary creation—to decipher their meanings beneficially. The interpretations, as they currently stand, coincide with humanity's scientific, intellectual, and spiritual progress.

32. In the Gospel of Thomas, Jesus is quoted as saying: "Perhaps people think that I have come to impose peace upon the world. They do not know that I have come to impose conflicts upon the earth: fire, sword, war."

33. It is granted that Jesus knew the structure, nature, and purpose of God-Creator's design. He understood that all things result from God-Creator's omni-love, omni-power, and omniscience. War is an initial stage of what eventually stimulates agreement, understanding, and peace.

34. By "imposing" conflicts Jesus would initiate ultimate peace or agreement. As he said, "I tell you that if two

of you on earth are in agreement about anything you ask for, it will be done for you by my Father in heaven. For, where two or three come together in my name there am I with them."[12]

35. In a perfect design by an omnipotent, pragmatically omni-loving God-Creator, any wars that occur should be seen as a necessary part of human progress toward agreement, peace, and progress toward godlikeness.

36. For humans to be godlike, we must go through an individual and collective process that draws out and cultivates the godlike qualities within us. These qualities cannot be realized, unless we go through the transformational process—which may include what we call pain, suffering, and wars as well.

37. To be godlike is to act out of omni-love and therefore possess the power of creation. It is to consistently align with the only real, influential powers of the universe. To be godlike is to be strong, creative, powerful, loving, and all that is good.

38. Where we see enmity, we block or weaken our alignment with God-Creator's power. Where we engage in war, we plainly exhibit our departures from godlikeness yet simultaneously propel ourselves forward toward godlikeness. The process is perceived as painful—As such, humans grow, learn from, progress, and eventually

overcome this unique behavior. Of course it is in our interest to avoid pain as much as possible. The more godlike people are, the less pain they experience.

39. In evolutionary creation, everything is in the process of becoming. When the element of time is removed from the analysis, it is easy to see that the entirety of the human journey toward godlikeness is essentially instantaneous.

40. For God-Creator, pleasure, happiness, pain, and suffering are all catalysts to propel humans toward godlikeness. Even conflict and war—where they exist—should be seen as necessary movements toward eventual agreement. Each person is driven by a primitive but divine guidance during each fight. It is a fight that cannot be left un-fought at that time. War and conflict elicit an intricate psychological process that ultimately fosters godlike qualities in people, such as compassion and love for fellow humans (and the desire to never do it again). Initial conflict also paves the way for mutual agreement, understanding of the other, and ultimately, peace.

41. All interactions should therefore be seen as originating from divine source. This week, practice recognizing that each person you encounter plays a unique and important role in God-Creator's design. No person, national or multinational organization, government, or event is

devoid of purpose; everything is perfectly intended for your, their, and God-Creator's benefit, progress, and joy. No matter who you are or where you are, this view can help you get the things in life that you desire. It's a perceptual shortcut to achieving anything you want, whether it's: happiness, money, love, or anything else.

42. If you currently view certain people or groups as enemies, try to understand why an omni-loving God-Creator would benevolently create and then place such a person or group in your path…for your own, theirs, and God-Creator's benefit. Ask yourself, where the opportunity rests in having this person or group in your life. In doing so you change your focus, alter your action, and create an inevitably beneficial sequence of events.

43. When you stop thinking of others as enemies but as divine entities placed in your path by an omni-loving God-Creator for your benefit, you act in accordance with the design. When you act in accordance with God-Creator's design, you act in harmony with (as opposed to against) the greatest benevolent powers of the universe. The immediate and long-term advantages of this are gigantic.

44. Each day identify the power in and implement Jesus Christ's teaching, "Love your enemy as yourself." This is a precise spiritual law that directly influences the material universe. Its application makes its rewards obvious.

45. The power, joy, and creative genius fostered by this law are harnessed only via its use. For it is impossible to sustain real and enormous success without the genuine support of others. Only full implementation of the law can ensure this.

PART IX

Fuel For Life: Super-Charge Your Closest Relationships

Quantum mechanics shows that two particles (photons of light or atoms) can become entangled with each other.

Entangled particles are connected in such a way that one particle always determines the properties of the other—even when the particles are physically far apart from each other.

The causes of entanglement will likely be discovered in the future, but for now the causes remain ambiguous. Some physicists theorize that the links between the particles are in another dimension, since these "linking forces" are not yet visible here.[1] Some physicists also theorize that the energy connecting the particles is too fast and too subtle to be detected, for now.

As science can tell so far, the laws that govern the quantum world (the world of the smallest particles) do not apply to the laws that govern larger things (such as material objects and people). That being said, similarities exist between these two realms of the design. Indeed, Kabbalah asserts that all levels of the universe are reflections of each other.[2]

Just as two particles affect each other from a distance once they become entangled, your closest relationships affect all aspects of your life. When your relationships are harmonious, their contentment fuels all life endeavors.

When relationships are disharmonious, they undoubtedly influence the results secured outside of the relationship—often not to your advantage.

Since all strength and support begins from our closest quarters and extends outwards from there, it is of vital importance that our closest relationships are healthy, strengthening, and empowering. This chapter explains the process in depth. It can help you find your life partner or heal stressed relationships....

PART IX

1. It is impossible to fully experience life's joy unless you have someone to share it with. Indeed, the highest

levels of joy are experienced in a person's most psychologically intimate relationships.

2. By design humans have an innate need to form and maintain close relationships with others.[3] Close relationships are the foundation from which joy, happiness, wealth, and fulfillment grow. Scientific research has shown that of all the people in your social network, your spouse or significant other will be the person that is most responsive to your needs.[4]

3. The greatest levels of affection, intimacy, and genuine support are found in marriage[5] and relationships of an equal (psychologically) intimate nature. For this reason, while all close relationships are of what we call divine origin, this chapter focuses primarily on those of a spousal nature. A person's life is arguably incomplete without the experience of this closeness to another.

4. Spousal relationships encourage enormous fulfillment, expansion, and growth. When you have been blessed with such a close relationship, its development should be one of your highest priorities.[6] These relationships form the groundwork for all of your other encounters. In this way they affect every aspect of your life and success.

5. In fact, the existence and quality of your closest relationships affect *every* (seemingly unrelated) interaction

outside of these close relationships.[7] Disharmony in one facet of life inevitably affects another: the closer the relationship, the larger the effect. For this reason the cultivation and maintenance of invigorating, supportive relationships is worth our most earnest attention. When these relationships are healthy and supportive it is much simpler to have, be, and do anything you want in life.

6. Frontier science has shown that all things dynamically influence each other. Strength in one place fosters strength in another. A full life of health, joy, creativity, and power begins with your closest relationships. It expands outwards from there.

7. Jewish mystics, or Kabbalists, convincingly state that all souls have a male and female half. These souls are split at their divine source, which causes them to be separate halves. Man and woman are incomplete—"half" entities—on their own. It is only by the union of these two halves that a complete or unified entity is formed.[8]

8. The material differences in form reflect the spiritual differences between the halves of male and female. Men and women function according to different physical, behavioral, and psychological mechanisms. They have different biochemical structures. When presented with the same external stimuli, different portions of their brains are activated.[9]

9. Men and women thus perceive and respond to reality in ways that are different but complimentary. To have intimate access to the other, via uniquely close relations, is to gain an inherent advantage over those who do not. Thus, close relationships cultivate greater achievement, growth, and personal power.

10. When a woman shares her thoughts with a man, she seeks intimacy via the nature of his response. If she feels understood, she classifies the encounter as more intimate in nature. Conversely, men rate intimacy based on *what* they have shared, as opposed to how the female responds.[10] Consequently, men and women process and interpret reality differently. Their unique structures provide them with different experiences of life.

11. Due to such intricate differences in reality processing, psychologically intimate relationships enable those involved to form a more complete construction of reality. These close relationships are one of the most pleasant catalysts for growth toward godlikeness. They foster increased understanding of omni-: love, support, success, power, and insight.

12. As the Zohar (Kabbalah scripture) explicates, spousal relationships generate complete spiritual union between two initially incomplete spiritual halves. Only by way of close union can each spirit reach its fulfillment and perfection. This manifests in many ways such

as being free from anxiety and depression, having lots of money to buy the perfect home, having the freedom to travel to exotic vacation spots, experiencing harmonious family and child relationships, and more…

13. As such, marriage and like relations are essential parts of an omni-loving God-Creator's design to help humans on their journey toward godlikeness. These relationships help us grow psychologically, emotionally, and spiritually. They thus propel humanity toward a state of godlikeness during which we humans are partners or *full* co-creators with God (see the prologue at the beginning of *A Guide to Your Supreme Power*).

14. Just as the pain of war and conflict elicit insight that ultimately increases godlikeness, pleasant and loving relationships increase godlikeness. All that exists is essential for our growth and development.

15. Intimate relationships benefit humans on many levels in God-Creator's design. People who are married (or in similar relationships) are shown to exhibit higher levels of overall health (both physically and mentally).[11]

16. This is because humans are biologically encoded with the desire to enter close relationships. Your physical body is designed so that the cells of your body are physically strengthened when you engage in psychological and physical closeness with your spouse or significant other.

17. This is evident even during the first stages of a special relationship. Nerve growth factor (NGF) is secreted at the outset of close relationships. NGF is a molecule that facilitates growth and survival of key nerve cells in your body. When the strengthening biochemical effects like those of NGF dissipate, other pleasurable chemicals such as oxytocin are released to foster more meaningful attachment and bonding.[12]

18. The biochemical oxytocin reduces anxiety and facilitates trust while inducing calmness and contentment. These empowering biochemical feelings influence your thoughts and behavior outside of your relationship. Harmonious marriages and similar relationships strengthen us at the level of our cell structure. These close relations also influence all of our thoughts and actions. It is thus imperative that these relationships be healthy in every way.

19. The Kabbalah makes clear that the healthiest relationships contain both the couple involved and the divine presence between them.[13] This is not to be taken literally. Instead, it is to remind you that the degree to which you act in accordance with God-Creator's design determines your happiness and fulfillment in every aspect of life. This is equally true in spousal relationships.

20. Highly advanced success and joy are dependent on knowing and recognizing God-Creator's design. Love is

the true language of God-Creator. When you love another person unconditionally, you enrich yourself and the other greatly. To love someone unconditionally is to align yourself with the power of God-Creator's omni-love. It is to connect with the source that directly influences the material realm; for love is an act not of the body but of the soul.

21. Only relationships based on unconditional love will foster superior mental and physical health. These relationships are the foundations for greater fulfillment in other aspects of life.

22. Where love is conditional, the relationship is destined to be painful—still a catalyst for growth toward godlikeness, but not a most pleasant one. That is because conditional love does not fully coincide with God-Creator's grand design.

23. Unconditional love demonstrates strength of character, whereas conditional love is closely aligned with a lack of strength. Conditional love is a more feeble force simply because it is selfish in nature. God-Creator's love is unconditional and benevolent.

24. Marriages and similar relationships that are based on unconditional love are in direct harmony with God-Creator's design. They therefore enable couples to experience godlikeness and profound joy. Conditional love is different.

25. A primary aspect of conditional love is the need to be sure that the relationship exhibits tangible equity. Keeping track of one's explicit rewards in close spousal relationships indicates a basic lack of security in the relationship.[14]

26. Only when one feels insecure in his or her place does he or she feel the need to be sure that tangible equity exists in a close relationship. In such instances one fears giving of him/her self unconditionally. This is a common defense mechanism but does not indicate a healthy relationship. All calculating behaviors detract from the quality of, and intimacy in, spousal relationships.[15]

27. Your closest relationships should contain strong foundations that enable each partner to freely give and express him/herself. It is a way to experience divine reality, growth, and fulfillment. When a person seeks confirmation of tangible rewards or equity in his or her relationships, he or she seeks to fulfill unrelated needs above all else.

28. When you intimately engage with another person for the purposes of meeting your own needs, you are mentally reducing the other person's rank to that of an instrument. Such action lacks integrity.

29. Where integrity is lacking, a loss of influence is too close behind. The universe is built on basic laws. It is known that all positions of influence require equivalent degrees of integrity.

30. Many intimate relationships are known to be conditional. Sometimes people attempt to use superficial intimacy as a means to distract themselves from more pervasive, personal, existential, or psychological dilemmas. These deeper tribulations are not effectively resolved with shallow solutions. False intimacy is an (inevitably unsuccessful) attempt to do just that.

31. Likewise, intimacy is not meant to be a safe place to intentionally disregard or harm others. In a universe designed by an omni-loving God-Creator, there is no such place.

32. We should never thoughtlessly or selfishly add the dimension of intimacy into our relationships. Psychological and physical closeness is a way to more closely align with God-Creator. When it is overused or under-regarded this divine connection is needlessly obscured.

33. Rebbe Menachem M. Schneerson wisely shared an old Jewish saying, "If you are close when you should be distant you will be distant when you should be close."[16]

34. To elaborate more explicitly, when you find yourself in what you believe to be a "divine relationship" of two corresponding souls, do not test the relationship by infidelity. While all things are ultimately for our and God-Creator's benefit, it is unintelligent that we should

knowingly make our experience more painful than pleasurable.

35. All spousal and similar relationships are designed to help people grow and advance toward godlikeness. Sometimes this requires communicating with your spouse about things that you would typically avoid discussing in general. When you transcend these self-imposed limitations your power increases everywhere outside of the relationship as well. Strength of any kind leads to greater strength. All strength increases happiness.

36. The Rebbe Menachem M. Schneerson often spoke beautifully of marriage and relationships. Tzvi Freeman's book, *Bringing Heaven Down to Earth*, shares the Rebbe's insight. Indeed, the Rebbe's wisdom concerning marriage should be translated to all close relationships:

Marriage is a microcosm of the soul's descent into this world: If you are here looking for what you can get out of this world, then the world's trappings will only drag you down. But if you are looking for what you can give, then you, your part of the world, and your soul are uplifted and filled with light. So too, when you enter a marriage: Look for what you can give, and reap harmony and love.[17]

37. When a person enters a relationship for the purpose of taking from another rather than giving from the heart, unless changes are made within that person, the relationship will not last. While this is not the sole

reason for frequent divorce, it is one of many. It is of course important to remember that all separations serve a divine purpose toward each person's ultimate benefit.

38. More than half of US and UK marriages now end in divorce.[18] However, since the universe functions in perfect order and harmony, all things occur for our highest development and benefit.

39. Even the relationships that do not last our entire lives or end in what we call pain are purposefully orchestrated by an omnipotent, omni-loving God-Creator for our benefit. They facilitate greater maturity and growth. As long as we interpret them as intentionally designed by an omni-loving God-Creator, they prepare us for and therefore benefit our subsequent relationships. (Where past relationships are viewed as negative, they inevitably encumber the intimacy and development of future relationships).

40. If a relationship ends, due to death or separation, it is important to remember the joy and growth that it gave you. It is fundamental to learn from these relationships. This ensures that you advance toward greater understanding, love, and all godlike qualities. We need only remember that all is divinely orchestrated for our benefit.

41. When you are in a close relationship, you need ask yourself just a few questions to accurately assess the degree of health and fulfillment that the relationship provides for both partners. It is best to meditate on these

questions, as opposed to intellectually deciding their answers. This ensures that you receive truthful insight. Do not rush to receive the answers to these deeper questions. Simply let them come to you throughout the week after you've meditated on them.

42. This week consider the following questions during meditation. You should consider those that are most applicable to you at this time. If you find that considering these questions is stressful or distressing, now is not the time to consider them. In such cases it is better to wait until you feel naturally compelled to reconsider them (perhaps after completing *A Guide to Your Supreme Power* ...or later) in a new light.

   a. Ask yourself if you believe that the person you are with can really help you reach your highest potential. Does your relationship foster growth for others who are outside of the relationship— or is the joy of the relationship confined strictly to the relationship itself?

   b. Do you unconditionally love this person, or are you using this relationship as a conditional means to satisfy unrelated needs?

   c. Do you make what you feel are often unreasonable concessions in this relationship? If so, why? Does this facilitate your highest growth?

d. Are you in any way breaching the integrity of this relationship? If so, why? How can you correct the situation to maintain your integrity? When will you do so?

e. Does your partner contribute to your growth in intangible ways that surpass what you can accomplish on your own? Is your relationship a beautiful, safe place where you feel a sense of total freedom and unwavering support?

f. In the event that you are not in a spousal (or similar) relationship at present, you may want to determine why that is the case as well as the degree of real contentment that gives you. Would you be willing to share a more intimate relationship with someone special, or are you intentionally withholding that aspect of growth from yourself for some reason? Have you been hurt previously in other relationships? Have you considered all of your past relationships as having been designed for your benefit by an omni-loving God-Creator?

43. The conditions for happiness vary greatly from person to person as do the nature of people's intimate relationships. Health and vibrancy in one facet of your life influence all of the other aspects of your life—either directly or indirectly. It is therefore important to be certain that when in close relations with a partner the

relationship exhibits perfect health, happiness, and fulfillment. When it does you are acting in harmony with God-Creator's design. This is a prime way to align with God-Creator's highest, most influential creative power. When people are in close spousal relationships, individual power is magnified by the couple's power. Indeed, "the whole is greater than the sum of its parts."

PART X

If You Want to Be Happy (and Successful), Don't Believe These Ideas

In a world designed by a pragmatically omni-loving, omnipotent God-Creator, all things serve a positive purpose. All things are designed to fuel the process of evolutionary creation (the human journey toward godlikeness).

Ideas and information are disseminated precisely when they are most beneficial for humanity. They are created (or discovered) and released only when they can help us to move forward in the most beneficial ways.

Even strongly endorsed ideas that we later realize are not entirely correct (such as the law of attraction as promoted by *The Secret* book) serve unique purposes, or they would not have existed. Such ideas are often catalysts for growth and development. They prompt us to question our knowledge and search for additional knowledge. Consequently, ultimate truth is eventually obtained.

This chapter addresses some of the recently circulating "mystical" ideas and discloses the verified mechanisms behind them. It thus contributes to the ongoing quest for truth—and a person is creative, powerful, and happy to the degree that he or she is acquainted with truth.

If you are to more comprehensively understand truth—the laws that guide the universe (and your life's outcomes)—Part X is essential. Because knowing these laws enables you to harness any amount of money you desire...get the career promotions you want...experience harmonious, loving partnerships...and radiate the joy of stress-free inner bliss...

PART X

1. Science is a methodical process by which humans uncover the laws and components of God-Creator's design. Many currently popular claims are based on misunderstandings of science and misinterpretations of their relationships to ancient wisdom. This can obviously be misleading.

2. We must be cautious that the claims we accept are based on accurate and current facts. What was scientifically

true yesterday is not necessarily true today and what is true today will not necessarily be true tomorrow.

3. By misleading and confusing the mind, incorrect or outdated claims produce incoherent thoughts and ineffective action (which can only limit our results). The acceptance of erroneous claims based on incomplete analysis must be avoided as much as possible.

4. Accurate or universally true knowledge enables us to think and act in accordance with the design. Where a person acts upon false conceptions, progress is hindered. Alignment with the design and its supportive power is lost.

5. All happiness, achievement, and fulfillment are gained by acting in accordance with God-Creator's design (as opposed to against it). This requires an understanding of universal laws.

6. For a law to be universal, it must produce the same result under the same parameters every time. If instances occur in which the "law" is fallible or its mechanism is incomplete, then it is not a law. This is the category under which the recently re-publicized "law of attraction" falls.

7. According to advocates of the law of attraction, each of your thoughts has a frequency and these frequencies are released into the universe, thereby attracting events and people on similar frequencies.

8. Although your thoughts are chemically charged, they do not directly emit frequencies that, in turn, attract events and people of similar frequencies to you. This is a misconception of the manner by which brain waves function.

9. Brain waves function as follows: Neurons (brain cells) communicate via synapses (passageways between cells) in your brain. This creates chemically-induced patterns of electrical activity. Different patterns characterize different states of consciousness.

10. Conscious states are characterized in terms of waves per second (wps), ranging from the normal waking state, with the most wps (beta state), to the sleeping state, with the least wps (delta state).[1] Alpha and theta waves describe states of consciousness between the waking and sleeping states—with theta waves indicating an essentially sleeping state.

11. You can intentionally direct your thoughts to influence (or change) your environment in your favor, but the mechanism is not one of mystical thought-frequency transmission. The processes are divinely designed and scientifically valid.

12. For example, the individual thoughts that you have and your consistent thought patterns determine the chemicals secreted by your brain. The neurons in your

brain (brain cells) become accustomed to the chemicals that are habitually secreted by your brain as a result of the thoughts you have.

13. Neurons soon become chemically dependent on the chemicals most often secreted by the brain.[2] In this way thoughts directly influence brain chemistry and soon restructure the brain.

14. Just as persistent thought patterns produce structural changes in your brain, they create structural changes in every cell of your body. Every thought you have produces a chain of chemical reactions in your body. The cells of your body become habituated to the chemicals most often secreted as a result of your typical thought patterns, influencing your physical health.

15. Your perspective determines your thought patterns. Your thought patterns determine the biochemicals released into your brain and body. These chemicals then cyclically influence your thoughts; thus, the mind and body perpetually influence each other.

16. Due to this cycle, perhaps it once appeared as though a certain type of thought "attracts" similar thoughts. This is likely the reason that law-of-attraction advocates assert that thoughts attract other similar thoughts to them[3]...and then attract events and people on those thought frequencies.

17. Such theories may have been credible (and correspondingly useful) in the past, but humanity has since progressed. Human reasoning, a manifestation of our imbedded intellect, has evolved. Additional knowledge has been discovered.

18. When you view all things as the result of the lawful design of an omni-loving, omnipotent God-Creator, your perception serves you. Your consequent thoughts soon enable you to interpret all that you encounter in a way that is favorable. Actions taken from this perspective inevitably influence your surrounding environment. You virtually, step by step, create a new reality and a new life for yourself and others. Every situation becomes advantageous.

19. By retraining your mind in accordance with this perspective, unconstructive thoughts disappear. All thoughts become constructive, useful, and powerful. With enough practice this becomes the natural—and most beneficial—way to respond to the events that constitute your reality. This method secures your success and fulfillment in all things. It gives you money, love, power….

20. These human psycho-biochemical-behavioral mechanisms constitute laws of God-Creator's design. For a law to be universal, its mechanisms must be the same in every instance.

21. One of the logical conclusions, for instance, according to the law of attraction is that Jewish people attracted the Holocaust to themselves—and all other persecutory occurrences in the world could be explained in this manner. Since thoughts do not emit frequencies as suggested by the law of attraction, the claim of attraction postulates the existence of evil or punishment among the victims.

22. In a system based on the concept of an omnipotent, omni-loving God-Creator, evil or punishment cannot exist. All occurrences in such a system serve the purpose of being ultimately good and should be evaluated from this perspective.

23. Persecutory events of immense atrocity (like war, ethnic cleansing, slavery, etc.) should be seen as catalysts for human development toward godlikeness. Both what we call pain and pleasure serve as motivating forces for individuals and societies toward godlikeness.

24. Events such as the Holocaust, slavery, and other such devastations have contributed to the growth of humanity toward godlikeness. History shows that both the victims and oppressors in such situations have evolved enormously as a result of these events. Humanity has, in turn, become more compassionate. It assumes more global responsibility for its individuals than ever before.

25. Incidents such as the Holocaust affect all of humanity. They are recorded in our conscious and subconscious minds. Their collective and individual psychological impacts are designed to ensure that the events will not happen again. Naturally, the process is gradual by our human standards. These occurrences directly propelled evolutionary creation forward to nobler heights of human development for at least half of the planet, so far.

26. It is likely that those who were persecuted and perished under circumstances like the Holocaust reached even higher levels of godlikeness than many others. Individuals who are persecuted have often attained greater awareness, compassion, and similarly powerful qualities that characterize godlikeness as a result of their suffering.

27. The Gospel of Thomas quotes one of the greatest teachers, Jesus Christ, accordingly. "Blessed are they who have been persecuted within themselves. It is they who have truly come to know the father."[4] Others soon grow more godlike, as well.

28. This is shown, for instance, via a note found near the Trans-Siberia railroad. A Holocaust victim wrote the note prior to his death. The note contained a prayer and also a letter to God. The person asked God to "forgive" those who had mistreated him and his family. He did not want God to "punish them" or make them suffer for

what they had done to him and his family. This individual had come to learn and master the universal law, "love your enemy as yourself." He was more godlike (creative, beautiful, powerful) than his persecutors.

29. It is important to remember that God-Creator's omni-love should be seen from a different perspective than human love. It is of a much wider or divine perspective. All things occur for God-Creator and humanity's benefit and progress toward godlikeness. Even the Holocaust, slavery, genocide and other painful events occur under the guidance of the pragmatically benevolent, omnipotent God-Creator. These events reflect humanity's evolutionary states during the process of growing toward godlikeness.

30. Prior to these collective experiences and our present state of knowledge, the law of attraction may have been deemed a reasonable explanation for much observable phenomena. At this stage of evolutionary creation, however, this law is outdated.

31. Ancient people knew even less of the physical and transcendental laws governing our universe than we do today. They knew less of their intricate relationships and the ways that they interacted. Ancient people therefore attributed most phenomena to mystical laws resembling the law of attraction. Stephen Hawking sums this up well:

In ancient times, the world must have seemed pretty arbitrary. Disasters such as floods or diseases must have seemed to happen without warning, or apparent reason. Primitive people attributed such natural phenomena, to a pantheon of gods and goddesses, who behaved in a capricious and whimsical way. There was no way to predict what they would do, and the only hope was to win favor by gifts or actions.[5]

32. The above quote enables us to better understand the origins of the ancient attraction idea. However, advocates of the law of attraction have more recently asserted that routine human thoughts create material reality at the quantum level. This is a basic misinterpretation of physics' quantum mechanics and the subatomic laws that determine God-Creator's design.

33. Frontier science has shown that the universe is comprised of energy. The subtler the energy field the more potent the energy—and the less humans know thus far.

34. Matter is comprised of atoms. Atoms are comprised of subatomic particles. Subatomic particles contain mostly "empty space." This empty space is known as the quantum field. The quantum field contains enormous energy and is becoming better understood by science.

35. The quantum field consists of subatomic particles that function in the form of either waves or particles. There is no distinction between particles and waves at this level. Waves are simply "probabilities" of potential

particles. Subatomic particles are therefore in a state of constant movement, changing from particles to waves and back again.

36. Frontier science has yet to precisely understand the laws of the quantum field beyond potential probabilities. This does not mean that precise laws do not cause what we currently understand as probabilities.

37. Einstein knew that God-Creator's universe functioned according to precise laws whether humans had already discovered these laws or not. "God does not play dice with the universe"[6] was his response to the idea that the quantum field was a realm of vacillating potential. He understood that precise laws determined the apparent probabilities that currently characterize what we know of the quantum realm.

38. Also, science cannot yet determine a subatomic particle's speed and position concurrently. It can only determine one or the other. When we know the speed, we do not know the position, and vice versa. This is referred to as the Uncertainty Principle. It is likely that both speed and position can be determined simultaneously, but our knowledge and tools are still insufficient.

39. When humans do not fully comprehend a phenomenon, they often deem it to be random, arbitrary, chaotic, or they think in terms of probability. Our lack of

understanding regarding quantum phenomena cannot be translated to mean that thoughts directly create physical reality at the quantum level. While this could potentially be the case, the facts remain unknown.

40. We must also keep in mind that the quantum field is probably not the definite field of Creation. Even more subtle, more potent fields likely exist beneath the quantum field that human science and its tools cannot yet detect.

41. For example, during a quantum leap, electrons are said to move instantaneously from one orbit to the next without ever entering the currently detectable space between the orbits.

42. One can conclude that during quantum leaps the electrons are entering an energy field that is too subtle for our current detection and analysis. It is therefore invisible to us. The process *appears* instantaneous. This subtler field could also be determining that which we now see as probabilities in the quantum field. As evolutionary creation progresses, so will science and its ability to unveil the intricacies of God-Creator's design.

43. The universe is energetic and coherent, and it functions according to precise laws on every level of existence. Where we have not yet discovered the precise mechanisms of God-Creator's design, we must be aware of our

limited knowledge and be careful not to leap to false conclusions. While certain ideas like the law of attraction once served humanity's benefit, advanced human knowledge and reasoning can no longer support this claim.

44. Progress toward godlikeness requires the removal of what we know to be inaccurate, needless, or untrue beliefs. Such beliefs prevent us from acting in accordance with God-Creator's design. They therefore hinder personal power and collective progress.

45. If we do not feed the mind with new knowledge, it tenaciously latches on to outmoded beliefs that can no longer serve us. The greatest creative genius stems from maintaining a perspective that is exceptionally receptive to new information. Clearly, all new information should be assessed for its validity before it is accepted as fact. If it is deemed valid, (constructive and beneficial), your mind has that much more to work with. Your possibilities grow exponentially.

46. This week enhance your creativity. You can do this by opening your mind. When a person thinks he or she knows all things regarding any given subject, he or she closes him/herself off to new knowledge; creativity is suspended and opportunities are equally limited (see also PART II). This makes it more difficult to make the money you want to make, drive the car you want to drive, or to transform your business for your benefit...

47. You can train your mind to cultivate creative genius when you realize that even the most frontier human knowledge is still vastly incomplete. We have much more to learn to be godlike. (Only God-Creator knows all things simply by virtue of being the Creator).

48. Focus on this truth prior to entering the silence this week: That even the most sophisticated human knowledge is still very limited. By internalizing this recognition, the mind becomes more receptive to previously unnoticed information. It begins seeking expansion instead of acting on the basis of already knowing. It begins to naturally acquire more knowledge. The results are: growth, power, and creativity as never before.

49. This world is comprised of energy. Nothing remains fixed. We are either moving forward in all things or we are regressing. The continuous acquisition of creativity-generating knowledge ensures that you advance. That is the purpose of this week's exercise.

PART XI

Become Immortal: Increase Energy, Youth, and Vibrancy

All success, advancement, and fulfillment require high levels of enduring energy. And our highest energy reserves are available to us only when the body and mind are in perfect health.

Potentially unconstructive thoughts and unhealthy lifestyle habits weaken the body and mind. In such cases the vibrant physical energy we are designed to exploit is the first resource to diminish.

With the right knowledge and perspectives, we can break potentially unhealthy habits and end the unconstructive cycles they fuel. This enables us to use our natural physical mechanisms to our advantage above all else.

For instance, Reactive Oxygen Species are the oxygen-containing molecules that react with the body's healthy molecules in a way that causes cellular damage[1] (and corresponding energy losses). With constructive perspectives and equally constructive lifestyle decisions, we can reinforce our natural antioxidant system to counteract these and other potentially damaging mechanisms.

That your levels of physical energy are totally within your control and influence is definite. Harnessing your most constructive powers and resources is entirely within your reach. You can heal physical pain, disease, and mental ailments….you need only utilize the most pertinent, updated knowledge for your advantage. This chapter is designed to provide you with the knowledge you need.

PART XI

1. The sensory illusion of uniform time encourages humans to think in a linear fashion. What we call life is often interpreted in linear terms with human birth being the beginning and human death being the end. The most basic sensory mechanisms of the human brain uphold this illusory thinking.

2. What is illusory is not true. The great teacher Jesus Christ (worshiped by many as a God or God in human image), sheds light on the true nature of life and death.

He suggests that the reality of existence transcends the temporary human physical form.

3. When confronted with questions of mortality, he said, "Have you discovered the beginning, that you are seeking the end? For where the beginning will be the end will be. Blessings on the one who stands at the beginning. That one will know the end and not taste death."

4. Jesus Christ affirms that the beginning and end are one and the same. Upon realizing one you find the other. Our true existence is immortal. It transcends human form and what we call birth and death. Upon realizing this you do not "taste" death or experience it via human sensory mechanisms.

5. Recognizing the true nature of existence gives you enormous power, the power to embrace your innate immortality as opposed to viewing existence solely in terms of your temporary human form. Upon realizing this true nature of existence, your perspective expands. Fear and other unconstructive feelings diminish or disappear, allowing you to design your life without their interference. You gain the power to fully embrace the freedom and joy of your current human form. Life becomes the beautiful celebration it was intended to be.

6. Your true nature is immortal. Of course this does not preclude you from enhancing the quality of life in

your current structure. The human form of existence is one of immense joy. It gives us an opportunity to mold and create the reality we desire—and contribute to God-Creator's creation in a meaningful and rewarding way.

7. A person's form is designed to be temporary. Sometimes people experience long-term illness or physical impairment by design. Such instances are catalysts for growth for all of humanity and should be viewed accordingly.

8. However, in most cases the physical form is intended to provide each person with maximum energy and vitality. When people age sometimes they do not feel as energetic as they once did. They may not be as healthy as they once were. This is due to a lack of knowledge regarding their human structure and God-Creator's design.

9. When you understand the meaning of immortality and the mechanisms by which the human body ages, you can influence the process to your benefit. While frontier science has only just begun to unravel the miracle of the human body's aging process, a wealth of information has already been discovered. It is exactly the information that we should know at this stage of our evolutionary creation (the human journey toward godlikeness).

10. For reasons greater than we can imagine (humanity is not yet godlike), the human body is not yet designed

(and may never be) to last forever. Aging appears to be embedded at the level of human DNA. The transience of the human form seems to be a vital aspect of God-Creator's design. Just as human physical life begins at the cellular level, so does its temporariness.

11. Each time a cell in the body divides, the new replication cell is less precise than the previous. This is because telomeres shorten every time a cell divides.[2] (Telomeres are regions of DNA that play a key role in the process of DNA replication.) Since telomeres themselves shorten with each cell division—and they are necessary for the cell division process—there is a limit to the number of times a cell can divide.

12. This mechanism incited the Telomerase Theory of Aging. Once scientists are able to decipher exactly what telomeres are responsible for regulating in the body, they will know the best hormonal supplement to assist the process, thereby extending longevity and life vitality.

13. While mechanisms for aging are embedded at the level of human DNA, unconstructive conscious or subconscious perspectives (and the emotions they produce) can accelerate the aging process. This occurs when a person's thoughts and perceptions produce "damaging" chemicals at the cellular level. Any damaging biochemicals resulting from unconstructive perspectives immediately affect the brain.

14. The hypothalamus is part of the brain. It guides the body's hormonal activity. With age, the hypothalamus can lose its ability to regulate hormones. Its mechanism becomes less effective. Frontier science suggests that the stress hormone cortisol is responsible for the hypothalamus losing effectiveness.

15. Each time a person experiences excessive stress, the adrenal glands produce excessive amounts of cortisol, adrenaline, and other potentially harmful hormones. These chemicals damage the hypothalamus, which causes it to produce more cortisol and like hormones. The negative effects of stress on the body are therefore cyclical.

16. All damaging negative emotions, including stress, are the result of perception. When you realize the essence of creation—that the universe is designed by an omni-loving, omnipotent God-Creator, your perception changes. Stress and other damaging emotions are reduced, if not eliminated entirely. When stress is reduced, so are its negative effects. The body ages gracefully and at much slower rates. Energy is constructively distributed throughout the body resulting in vitality and strength.

17. During our current stage of evolutionary creation, we have available many resources to support health, energy, and physical strength throughout a person's entire life. To be vital, energetic, strong, healthy, and creative is to be godlike. Recognition of and alignment with God-Creator's design

is preliminary for all godlike attributes. When guided by (recognition of and alignment with) God-Creator's design, anything that you find contributes to your highest health, performance, and well-being should be used.

18. For example, many people endorse frequent but low-dose human growth hormone (HGH) injections. HGH was not originally intended to rejuvenate people during the aging process, but it is sometimes prescribed for this purpose. When used for longevity, HGH is shown to decrease body fat, increase muscle mass, strengthen bones, improve oxygen consumption (cells rely on oxygen for vitality and life), and increase physical health during the aging process.[3] The body, in essence, becomes younger.

19. Improving longevity is still a fairly new use for HGH. Debate and controversy continue to surround the subject—HGH is currently available via medical prescription only. When you are consistently aligned with the harmony of God-Creator's design, you accurately assess all things—including that which is most beneficial for your health and energy on your journey toward godlikeness.

20. While compensatory support can be helpful, the vibrant functioning of your cells is significantly dictated by lifestyle choices. For example, it has long been known that overeating does not contribute to health or high energy levels. It does just the opposite. When you

overfeed the cells of your body, they divide faster. Cells have an embedded limit on the number of times they can divide—fifty or more divisions are the estimates. By eating less the cells divide slower. This improves energy, appearance, and longevity. Physical energy begins at the biochemical, cellular level.

21. A healthy, energetic biochemical and physical state translates into a constructive, productive mental state. This enables you to recognize God-Creator's design and function accordingly. Disturbances, such as fatigue, depression, anxiety, and emotional distress, can result from cell toxicity and unhealthy lifestyle habits. It is therefore of great importance that you condition your biochemistry to serve you rather than work against you. Consistent recognition of God-Creator's grand design promotes just that.

22. Creative power requires an optimally coherent cell structure for its full manifestation. An unhealthy diet does not foster cellular coherence (see also Part IV). Poor diet choices and unconstructive lifestyle habits disrupt coherence by contributing to the production of free radicals in the body.

23. A free radical is a molecule that has a free electron. These molecules react to the body's healthy molecules in a destructive manner. They attack cell membranes causing the cell to create metabolic waste. This creates toxicity.

All cell toxicity reduces energy, strength, and cellular vitality.

24. Antioxidants stabilize free radicals, thus removing their ability to induce toxicity. Antioxidants are present in all vibrantly colored fruits and vegetables. Supplement antioxidants, such as alpha-lipoic acid and DMAE, can be taken as additional protection against free-radical-induced cellular damage. Research shows that alpha-lipoic acid is four hundred times more powerful than vitamin E and C combined. DMAE improves mood and memory in addition to strengthening cell membranes. Assess this information and use it for your physical wellness and advantage.

25. Antioxidants significantly reduce the toxicity induced by free radicals. However, it is ultimately constructive, health-inducing lifestyle choices that contribute most to maintaining vibrant cellular energy.

26. High energy levels and the momentous achievements they generate require that you maintain a toxic free cell structure. When you understand God-Creator's benevolent design, you no longer crave toxin-inducing substances. When a person experiences the enormous pleasure of aligning with creative power (and its benefits), he/she is careful not to weaken or obstruct it. And toxins reduce this alignment while also shortening our endurance.

27. Toxicity creates acidic waste in cells. Nobel Prize winner Dr. Alexis Carrel showed that when toxins are completely removed from an organism's cells the cells can tentatively live forever.[4] A nutrient-rich, water-based diet that is primarily alkaline (as opposed to acidic) significantly reduces toxic acidity.

28. Toxicity and cellular acid reduce physical energy and can eventually produce illness. Insufficient energy or a lack of health affects every aspect of a person's life. The more we understand toxicity, the more we can reduce it. The result is increased energy levels, longevity, and a higher quality of life. And increased energy means having the vitality to live, love, laugh, and play with the people who matter to you most....

29. It is shown that, sometimes, with age, cell membranes become more solid. This can create a toxic accumulation called lipofuscin inside the cell. Sometimes aging or liver spots contain lipofuscin. Frontier science has shown that easily accessible supplements reduce the presence of lipofuscin in cells. Some of the more effective supplements are DMAE and Acetyl-L-Carnitine. There are also conventional (prescription) medications that reduce lipofuscin.

30. God-Creator's design is such that nothing functions in isolation. All features of the design influence the working whole. It is thus important to keep all aspects

of your body thriving at the cellular level...this facilitates full body health. Vibrancy and power begin at this smallest level and extend outward from there—to all avenues of your life. The ever-present power of God-Creator's design is here for your advantage.

31. Even our cells contain powerhouses. These powerhouses are defined as mitochondria. Mitochondria create ATP (Adenosine Triphosphate), which is the chemical that provides energy for every single thing you do. When mitochondria incur free radical damage due to overeating or cell toxicity, they provide the body with less ATP. The result is less energy, vigor, and vitality. Antioxidants protect these powerhouses from free radical damage or oxidation, thus enhancing ATP production—and increasing energy.

32. God-Creator's design is intricate. Frontier science has only begun to discover its individual components. The laws of the design demonstrate that you cannot affect one component of the design without affecting all others. For this reason you should be well informed about any medications or supplements you choose to take. Some may be helpful and others less so. When you act in accordance with God-Creator's design, you make the most beneficial choices to maximize energy, vitality, health, and well-being.

33. Certain exercises like yoga are unique in that they address both physical and mental-emotional health. Yoga

is a holistic method for increasing flexibility, energy, and stabilizing weight, while improving sleep and immunity and regulating cholesterol.[5]

34. By stabilizing the nervous system, yoga exercises immediately reduce stress. Yoga is shown to have long-term benefits, such as releasing anxiety, depression, and hostility, while immediately increasing both physical and emotional endurance. The multi-faceted benefits of yoga make it well worth practicing. Even the breathing aspects of yoga help to clean the lymph system, which is the body's primary purification system.[6] (The lymph system strongly influences overall health and strength).

35. Every cell in your body is surrounded by lymph. Yogic breathing helps you cleanse your body at this level, while increasing energy, stamina, and overall vitality. The greatest effectiveness of yoga lies in the fact that your entire being (mental and physical) can be revived in a matter of minutes. (You can access free yoga exercise resources from Power Yoga instructor, Bryan Kest, at: www.TheOneWorldInitiative.com/yoga.html).

36. Physical exercise can also enormously increase energy and well-being, while increasing the growth of neural stem cells in your brain.[7] Exercise releases endorphins into the brain, which makes people feel happy and emotionally balanced. If you want to access one of your body's greatest energy reserves during exercise, you

should condition your body to burn fat. Eighty-five percent of the body's energy is stored in fat, so this is your most enduring energy reserve.[8]

37. Most people obtain their energy by burning sugar. The energy provided by sugar is short-lived. Once it is burned, a person craves more, and a cycle of burning sugar is perpetuated. When the body relies on sugar for energy, the result is emotional-mental instability and loss of alignment with God-Creator's design on the cellular and mental levels.

38. You can train your body to burn fat instead of sugar by exercising more slowly. Most people exercise strenuously or intensely for short durations. The result is an immediate burning of sugar, followed by emotional instability and more craving for sweets. Thus, the body becomes trained to rely on sugar as its primary source of energy. Research shows that slow exercises such as walking condition the body to utilize fat (instead of sugar) for energy.[9] The result is high, enduring energy and balanced, feel-good vitality.

39. When healthy, the human body is designed to be able to live in excess of one hundred twenty years. A perceptual recognition of God-Creator's design and the cellular coherence it fosters allows you to live a healthy, dynamic, and full life. Life is designed to gracefully transform, not with illness or disease, but with total style.

You are meant to have high energy so you can travel to your dream vacation spots with your loved ones and prosper in every way.

40. An omni-loving God-Creator's perfect creation was not designed for people to be ill during their lives. Illness or potentially uncomfortable aging is simply a catalyst for human growth in evolutionary creation; it is a catalyst to seek solutions. It is a chance to research and unveil the secrets of creation while employing the human spirit and intellect via science. It is also a prompt to better understand our natural human health mechanisms in our journey toward a godlike state.

41. As evolutionary creation and science progress, life extension will advance as well. Advances such as nanomedicine and gene therapy research have already begun and are expected to help people live better into later years—for all their years.

42. Nanomedicine in particular is a study of medicine that focuses on manipulating matter at the atomic and molecular scales. It is expected to eventually have the ability to repair cellular damage (on a molecular level) that is caused by unhealthy aging.

43. Gene therapy can be used to replace mutated genes with healthy genes to reverse unhealthy aging. Cloning and stem cell research can contribute to the replacement

of damaged cells with new, healthier cells. Indeed, science has only just begun its quest for life extension and healthy, up-to-the-minute living; (see also the discussion on science and its relationship to the Tree of Knowledge in Part VII).

44. Those who maintain perfect cellular health have an enormous advantage in all things over those who do not. For this reason maintaining a healthy lifestyle that is in sync with the design is highly beneficial.

45. When you go into the silence, you synchronize the cells of your being with God-Creator's design. It is shown that after just a few months those who meditate have the biological structure of a person who is five to twelve and twenty years younger.[10] You can just imagine how these benefits exponentially increase when you not only meditate but also practice yoga and recognize the perspectives in *A Guide to Your Supreme Power*.

46. This week decide what you wish to improve or reinforce regarding your physical health. When in the silence, assert these conditions as already existing facts. In doing so you activate all the power of your mind and body to bring about the conditions you desire. Your actions will soon sustain these decisions.

47. By retraining your mind in the silence, you create new thought patterns, reduce your biological age, and

synchronize all your cells and DNA with God-Creator's design…but most importantly you sow the seeds required for healthier behavioral changes (which translates into even better results).

48. Retraining your mind in the silence will prompt you to begin the new habits necessary to manifest your desired physical condition. In the silence you quiet your being and directly influence your mind's seat of all mundane decision—and it is our moment-by-moment choices that cumulatively create energy, health, vigor, vitality, and strength, or their opposites.

PART XII

What Every Great Leader and Statesman Knows

Just as your life at any given moment is a reflection of yourself at that time, a society is a reflection of its people. This includes its social, political, religious, and economic structures.

Every society is designed to respond to apparently conflicting pressures of various sizes during the course of evolutionary creation. These pressures (religious, economic, political, etc.) induce changes that fuel a society toward greater advancement; toward greater godlikeness.

Of course the manner by which a people respond to such pressures demonstrates their current level of godlikeness. Where we see godlikeness, we see creative solutions holistically implemented for the good of all, and vice versa.

This chapter discusses the design behind our collective creations (our societies) and the ways that we tend to respond to their inherent pressures. As no one exists in a vacuum, this investigation is well worth our attention.

For, only by understanding the true dynamics of an entity can you influence its mechanisms for your benefits. This means being able to earn more money, transform your business, promote your career, and achieve more overall life fulfillment within your social structure, while being happy and healthy in every way.

PART XII

1. We know that the human body is precisely designed according to intricate laws, but humans cannot yet design it themselves outside of procreation. Advanced knowledge and growth toward godlikeness is required.

2. We also know the primary elements that comprise the human body are oxygen, carbon, hydrogen, nitrogen, calcium, and phosphorous. These six elements make up 99 percent of the human body.[1] They are the same elements that comprise 99 percent of all living matter on earth.

3. All matter contains the same chemical elements as earth. The idea that God-Creator created Adam from the earth's soil is an accurate but simplified truth. (The Hebrew word for soil is *adama*).

4. The Bible's metaphorical language is designed to state universal truth in a way that can be understood by humans in accordance with their stage of evolutionary creation. It is written in several dimensions and is encrypted.

5. Had the Bible one-dimensionally explained the precise scientific mechanisms by which the universe was formed, it would have been discarded. This information would have been beyond the intellectual capacity of our biblical ancestors. Even today we would be greatly confused by this information. Knowledge is presented only when humanity has progressed enough to constructively utilize it.

6. All scientific knowledge coincides with our level of godlikeness. Physicists state that the body is made of atoms. It is known that these atoms are 99.9 percent empty void or space. This space is considered empty, likely because human tools and intellect cannot yet decipher these subtle fields. It is known that the more subtle the energy field, the more potent the energy in it. However, that which we cannot detect does not yet exist for us. This does not mean it is not an integral part of our existence.

7. Any new knowledge requires an equivalent degree of godlikeness on the part of humans lest it be improperly implemented. The existence of nuclear weapons

indicates this basic truth. As a pragmatically omni-loving, purpose-driven God-Creator, it is in God-Creator's divine interest that the act of creation realizes completion.

8. It is known that God created humankind in "its own image and likeness." The act of creation is still in progress (thus, the term "evolutionary creation"). Humans are in the process of reaching the state of godlikeness. The closer one's progression toward godlikeness, the more tools and information are available…the happier and more joyful that person is and the more outstanding are his or her accomplishments and contributions.

9. Although we collectively do not fully understand God-Creator's creation, we know more than those who lived prior to us. We have built upon and expanded their knowledge. The civilization that we live in reflects this.

10. Any private, political, and social institutions fashioned by a group of people directly reflect that people's level of growth toward godlikeness. Progression toward godlikeness (creativity, strength, power, love, etc.) begins at the level of individuals and extends outward from there—to their nations and beyond.

11. Like all civilizations, the civilization inhabited by Jesus Christ reflected the collective godlikeness of its people at that time. It was often a violent society, based on forceful threat as opposed to godlike power.

12. It was this violent civilization that crucified its political opponents, one of whom was Jesus Christ. That lineage of humanity has since progressed.

13. Christianity, as preached by Jesus, was initially a "deviant" sect of Judaism. Jesus acquired an original following of over three thousand people. This religion was initially confused with Judaism, since they were so similar in thought. With the work of the Apostle Paul and his missionaries, Christianity established itself as an accepted religion.[2]

14. Members of Christianity were often persecuted—as has been the case with many religions. This was the situation with Christians in Palestine and Rome until Constantine the Great ended their persecution. Like all civilizations, Rome's many justices and injustices, perfections and shortcomings reflected the growth and progress of its civilians at that time.

15. Albeit Rome's "higher" development, soon more primitive Germanic tribes overtook the empire. Thus began Europe's Middle Ages. The Romans did however "give" the Germanic tribes a special gift: Christianity (a belief in one source of creation: monotheism). Like all peoples, the manner by which Germanic tribes interpreted Christianity and implemented its practice in Medieval Europe reflected their level of godlikeness.

16. Humanity has since seen much violence and primitive action in the name of religion. It is not the religions themselves that contain these ideas but a people's evolutionary interpretation of them. As we progress toward godlikeness, so do our interpretations of all things, including divine understandings.

17. The present and historical misgivings of any organized religion are merely reflections of the intellectual progress of its people (leaders and those who are led). In a world designed by a pragmatically omni-loving, omnipotent God-Creator, all things serve a beneficial purpose for individual growth toward godlikeness. The social contract in particular plays a significant role in this process. We would like to briefly discuss this subject to provide an expanded understanding of the design.

18. The first known social contract was between God-Creator and Abraham. This and subsequent contracts with God-Creator form the basis of our civilization today. The Church helped to foster the implementation of these contracts, until society grew godlike enough for the separation of church and state. It is here that social contracts became more sophisticated.

19. For people to become more godlike, social contract is needed. This fundamental arrangement is simply a manifestation of the perfect order upon which the universe functions. It is God-Creator prompting its creation forward.

20. Any social contract is simply a reflection of the people who created it and live within its guidelines.

21. Even the most primitive social contract requires that a person overcome his or her more selfish nature to better consider others. History shows that, in their most undeveloped form humans can be self-centered. Anything that is to be constructive requires a departure from this view. No enduring achievement is the result of self-centered motives. It may sometimes appear this way, but a deeper look will always reveal the opposite.

22. With social contracts people form and become part of a meaningful society, while still preserving their individuality, the rewards of which are vastly superior to anything a human can do on his or her own. The only way to live harmoniously with others, thus far, is via social contract or agreement. All social agreements protect the individuals of the society and are upheld by a ruler or political body. The social contract should be based on the law "Love your neighbor or enemy as yourself." This is the only way to ensure its holistic, enduring power.

23. Many notions of the ideal social contract have evolved throughout history. Each is a distinct reflection of the author's individual insight and intellectual development—in accordance with a fair observation of those around him or her.

24. For example, Thomas Hobbes first detailed the contract theory suggesting that humans, given their quite primitive nature at that time, would enter a social contract solely out of selfish interests. We now know that it is in a person's higher interests not to act from his or her most selfish nature. In this manner that person gains true power.

25. Later, Locke's ideas for social contract emphasized the protection of the individual, a person's property, and his or her body.[3] These basic requirements reflect the very fundamental needs for social agreement during his time.

26. Rousseau of the Enlightenment had a still more optimistic view, judging that humans could be nurtured from birth to be selfless. He suggested that a social contract could be implemented when individuals relinquished a degree of individual freedom in favor of the holistic common good.

27. These and similar social contract theories have come to further influence and form the foundation of modern day society. Judeo-Christian morals, in particular, heavily influence Western democratic social contracts. The US president stands beneath the words, "In God We Trust," each time he addresses the nation. Members of the US House see a statue of Moses holding the Ten Commandments each working day.[4]

28. Like any other time period, our current democracy-republic and its institutions directly reflect the growth of its individuals. Much of this growth sprouted from what are now internalized, monotheistic ideals and philosophy.

29. Monotheism forms the deepest foundation of all Western civilization. Western democracy is simply a governing construct of a monotheistic people. As Western-style democracy spreads, so do the seeds of monotheism upon which it stands, and Abraham's philosophical descendants (monotheists) are *multiplied beyond number, like the stars in the sky and the sand on the seashore*[5]—a feature of evolutionary creation prophesied in the Bible.

30. We overtly saw this feature of evolutionary creation take place when democratic ideology overcame Soviet Communism—without the need for outright war. We see this taking place again in the Middle East. Except now the Internet and its fast communication forums are helping spread monotheism-based, democratic ideals even more peacefully. The ideological and cultural influences go both ways.

31. Another chief democratic ideal is the free-market economy. Just as democracy is a construct of monotheistic people, so are democratic economic principles—which China has recently adopted somewhat differently. As these unifying global changes take place, we progress

closer toward the state of agreement or heaven as mentioned by Jesus Christ.

32. In many cases we see transformation and change occurring more peacefully than before. This ability to overcome conflict and incite transformation without war demonstrates a level of godlikeness on the part of humanity. While the process of evolutionary creation appears to be lengthy (many centuries long), it is likely happening instantaneously for God-Creator due to time relativity. As we progress, so do our social contracts, societies, and the methods by which we govern them.

33. Just as the unique arrangement of your life at any moment is a reflection of yourself, a society is an echo of its people. The society in which you live and its institutions directly express the individual developments of the people that live there.

34. The private sector, political sector, public service, and all industries demonstrate the growth of a society's people. In accordance with evolutionary creation, it is the individual people that create these things. This is a people's way of expressing their creative power—which as yet differs from the creative abilities characteristic of higher godlike states.

35. Where the people are intellectually or emotionally primitive, the society is growing and could potentially

be defined as corrupt and largely unconstructive. Where the people are intellectually and emotionally advanced, the society is harmonious and prosperous in every way.

36. Any imperfection, violence, or corruption in a society indicates a low degree of godlikeness amongst its individuals. Where all people are godlike, heaven or the state of agreement as mentioned by Jesus Christ exists.

37. A change in any institution first requires a change at the level of the individual. When individuals are more godlike, they are more creative, successful, happy, and fulfilled. Their social creations function with perfect, constructive ease. It is therefore of great importance to advance the individuals of a society so the society can advance.

38. All scandal, corruption, or catastrophe at the social level is a catalyst for individual and collective advancement. No incident or individual exists in isolation; every aspect of the social body is an explicit reflection of the whole—its perfections and imperfections, its strengths and weaknesses.

39. A society's response to any catalyst reflects its present stage of development in the process of evolutionary creation (the human journey toward godlikeness). So far, history shows that we respond to catalysts—such as scandal, corruption or catastrophe—first emotionally, then intellectually. The result is typically an increase

in regulations that are inherently limited, as are all unholistic responses.

40. Over-regulation is a fear-driven response often based only on technical information. Humans are designed to progress forward in evolutionary creation. This often causes them to find all potential and, ultimately, mutually beneficial loopholes in humanity's regulatory acts. For instance, the entire Wikileaks organization and many other legally functioning ventures are exclusively constructed via and run by means of regulatory loopholes.

41. It is known that lobbyists like Jack Abramoff could not have prospered in a society that does not prompt and underhandedly endorse such action. Companies like Enron were similarly driven to act in an unlawful manner—implicitly or explicitly. Eliot Spitzer's resignation brought to light equally intangible flaws within the social body, illuminating its individuals' need to grow toward greater godlikeness.

42. The 2007–2008 financial meltdown, the shift from traditional lending to high-risk lending implemented by Fannie Mae, and NYSE insider trading, are basic reflections of our current, individual states of godlikeness.

43. The ways that people respond to the natural pressures of their social structure reflect their level of

godlikeness. The cumulative results of these responses constitute our society.

44. Where creative solutions that coincide with God-Creator's design are implemented in response to market or political pressures, the results are beneficial over the long and short terms. People are happier, they make more money, they live more comfortable, luxurious lives...However, where solutions based on panic, fear, or ego mechanisms are implemented in response to these pressures, the results are soon what we call painful (people have less money and less individual contentment).

45. In a world designed by an omni-loving, omnipotent God-Creator, painful results are simply prompts for higher development. They are catalysts for growth toward godlikeness.

46. The formation of the United Nations (UN) was a reaction to the painful catalyst of World War II. With benevolent aims that include the development of all countries and world peace, the UN mirrors the godlikeness of its leaders and the world's peoples. As individuals further develop toward greater godlikeness (creativity, power, love, etc.), the UN will reflect these changes. The day shall come when the mere idea of war will be a relic of previous times. Such measures will no longer coincide with the collective godlikeness of this planet's people. Further growth is required.

47. In a world of inextricable connections, no (global or local) event is independent of the individual. Every aspect of society is a reflection of its individuals. He or she who understands this is given enduring creative power; he or she is more advanced in godlikeness. These are the people who often embody the qualities of statesmanship and leadership.

48. This week recognize that there are no isolated entities. Every single person, event, and occurrence is a reflection of the whole (directly or indirectly). The Buddha understood this truth well, and many people have spent much of their lives trying to fully comprehend it as he did. There is a reason for this.

49. The simple recognition of God-Creator's creation as one cohesively functioning entity contains enormous power. It enables you to see the relationships between all things. This is the fount of creative genius.

50. God-Creator designed the world as a single creation. Each aspect is of divine importance or it would not exist. Any apparent differences that can result in dispute are simply catalysts for further development and growth toward godlikeness. This is the case at both the individual and global levels.

51. All perfections and imperfections, agreement and disagreement are manifestations of the collective entity

as it currently exists and functions. Where one component of the whole is improved, the rest is positively influenced; in this way the world progresses.

52. Progress toward godlikeness thus begins with the individual and expands accordingly. It is therefore of great importance that all leaders and individuals attain the highest possible levels of godlikeness. This ensures enduring success in all things. The world responds to individual godlikeness with only favor and benevolence.

53. As you enter the silence this week, take your time and dive into a new stratum. Try to understand God-Creator's holistic entity. Pierce its layers of knowledge as deeply as you can. As you do so, mundanely isolated judgments will cease, and you will begin to see the beauty of connectivity and integrity in all things. You will see that all things are intricately connected—that no single thing can exist apart from the whole of creation.

54. When you recognize that each thing is a reflection of the one functioning whole, you do more than synchronize yourself with the power of God-Creator's design; you become indistinguishable from it.

PART XIII

Transform Your Negative Emotions Into Assets

Emotions always influence a person's thought processes to a greater or lesser degree. In fact, there is no such thing as purely rational (emotion-free) thought. Rational and emotional thought are considered separately only for the purposes of human study.

Investment theories based on purely rational cost-benefit analysis are, therefore, largely incomplete. These theories fail to consider the highly influential emotional processes that underlie all decision-making.[1] Research shows that emotions significantly influence our decisions—particularly when these decisions contain high degrees of risk or uncertainty.[2]

The more complex or subjectively important the decision, the greater a person is emotionally influenced.[3] In these and many other ways, the biochemical effects of our emotions influence all of our thoughts and actions

Where thoughts are constructive, our emotions serve us. Where they are unconstructive, we restrict ourselves from creativity, superior performance, and the ability to achieve extraordinary results.

It is to our great advantage to understand, decode, and influence the activity of our emotions for our benefits. Understanding these processes can be the difference between being able to seize life's opportunities, or unfortunately, missing them. This chapter highlights the most powerful mechanisms involved.

PART XIII

1. The most advanced Kabbalah scholars state that all things function according to precise laws as designed by God-Creator. Even internal phenomena like emotions serve an indispensable purpose in the whole of God-Creator's design. They are driven by law.[4]

2. Emotions play a key role in evolutionary creation (the human journey toward godlikeness) or they would not exist. These mental phenomena appear to be primitive, random, or chaotic only when we lack knowledge of the basic laws that govern them.

3. Most people agree that our emotions are subjective, inner experiences that influence all our mental processes and behavior.[5] However, they are such an elaborate part of human consciousness that scientists have yet to agree on a precise definition for the word "emotion."[6]

4. While science has not yet discovered all the laws that govern human emotion or devised a standard definition, many important mechanisms that underlie emotional processes have already been unveiled.

5. Your emotional states determine what your brain registers and how that information is interpreted. Similarly your interpretations of events and other people determine your emotions. As such, the process that generates your emotions is cyclical. Your emotions directly influence your actions and the results they produce. Attention, motivation, and behavior are strongly influenced by emotional phenomena.[7]

6. As primary determinants of human experience and behavior, the mechanisms underlying emotion are well worth our attention. By understanding the laws that govern these phenomena, we can utilize their processes for our benefit. For instance, when our emotions are positive we act in ways that generate wealth, harmonious relationships, and the happiness these things bring...this requires mental power.

7. The human brain is unable to absorb every bit of information with which it is presented. It therefore only retrieves information that matters to a person. Information matters to the extent that it ignites emotion circuits in the brain.[8] The emotion circuits that promote information absorption can range anywhere from mild curiosity to elation or anxiety.[9] Far more than elation or anxiety, over three thousand words exist to describe the many different emotions we experience.[10]

8. Since all accumulated knowledge in the brain is connected—directly or indirectly—to emotion circuits, there is no such thing as purely rational thought. The element of emotion always influences perception, thought, and action to a greater or lesser degree.

9. The neural mechanisms in the brain that govern rational thought and emotions are entirely interconnected. The distinction between rational thought and emotional process exists solely for the purpose of human study. Science must conceive of and study each process in isolation (rational vs emotional) only to better comprehend the functioning whole. This is how humans unveil the various components of God-Creator's design. When the functioning whole of God-Creator's design is understood in entirety, we will have reached collective godlikeness.

10. Indeed, all aspects of the design function together. For example, when the biochemistry of your body is

healthy and balanced, emotions are constructive. Where toxicity or imbalance exists in the body, emotions are unconstructive and pose challenges for productive thought. Emotions are the products of both biochemical and psychological mechanisms.[11]

11. When you recognize that an omni-loving, omnipotent God-Creator designed our orderly, purpose-driven world, you prompt beneficial psychological processes that help produce positive emotions. This means that you see all things as coherent, constructive, and advantageous for development; all things are productive and definitely good. You dive into deeper strata of the design and see the inner connections. With this view your emotional states are activated in kind.

12. Our interpretations of events create our emotional states, which, in turn, activate biochemicals. These biochemicals can take the form of hormones, neurotransmitters (brain chemicals), and enzymes in the body. As hormones they enter the blood and affect your organs. As neurotransmitters they help the neurons in your brain communicate. As enzymes they metabolize substances generated within and outside of the body.[12] Emotional states affect all biochemical processes and therefore all aspects of your physical well-being.

13. During periods of mental stress or negative emotion, your body releases hormones, such as cortisol,

adrenaline, and norepinephrine. While all aspects of God-Creator's design are ultimately constructive, creating an internal excess of these chemicals does not serve your immediate interests, power, or health. Excess feelings of stress are catalysts for growth; they signal (via pain) that greater knowledge of and harmony with God-Creator's design is required.

14. When hormones such as cortisol and adrenaline are released, your immune[13] and digestive systems temporarily suspend themselves. Energy resources are depleted, and heart rate increases along with blood pressure. The homeostasis or balance of the body is interrupted. If stress hormones are consistently present in excess, the results are hypertension, potential cell mutation, and a myriad of stress-related health problems.

15. Most hormones are not necessarily stress-related. They are beneficial to health, overall strength, and well-being. They facilitate balance in the body's organs and enable intracellular communication. Hormones, in and of themselves, contribute to life. When your emotions are positive and aligned with God-Creator's design, their related hormonal substrates serve you.

16. In God-Creator's design, all things function in perfect order. Everything is intricately connected. Nothing functions in isolation. By positively affecting one aspect of a thing, you positively affect all others.

17. Emotions, physical health, thought, and behavior function in coherent unison. Hormone levels affect neurotransmitter functioning and vice versa. When hormones are released as a result of stress, the brain does not release sufficient levels of important neurotransmitters like serotonin in response.

18. Serotonin is a neurotransmitter that induces feelings of happiness. Like the brain chemical GABA, it reduces anxiety and depression. When serotonin is adequately present in your brain, you have high energy and few sleep disturbances among many other feelings of well-being.[14] Maintaining a focus that synchronizes with the beauty and creativity of God-Creator's design fosters the release of neurotransmitters (and hormones) that coincide with your higher interests, happiness, and goals. This translates into more fulfilling relationships, making more money, and creating the life you've always wanted.

19. In addition to acting in coherent unison with each other, some biochemicals serve multiple functions. For example, epinephrine (also known as adrenaline) functions as a hormone and neurotransmitter. In excess, epinephrine causes anxiety, sleeplessness, and over-excitation. Deficient levels are characterized by lack of mental focus and fatigue[15]... this means performance declines and opportunities are missed.

20. Serotonin, epinephrine, and all mood-regulating neurotransmitters are released in perfect precision in the most constructive amounts when your perspective coincides with God-Creator's design. By viewing reality in sync with God-Creator's design, you align your entire being with its power and creative genius. Thus, emotions gain constructive momentum and serve you in the best ways possible.

21. Your emotions influence all cellular, chemical, energy, and thought processes of your being. They determine (and indicate) the extent to which you are aligned with the divine forces of the universe. It is obviously to your great advantage to maintain a coherent perspective that elicits genuinely powerful, positive emotions.

22. In a world designed by an omni-loving God-Creator, all aspects of the design serve your growth and development toward godlikeness. By recognizing this basic actuality, you harness the power of God-Creator's design for your human efforts. You work in unison with God-Creator as opposed to working against the supreme powers of its designed laws—emotions included.

23. All aspects of God-Creator's design are meant to serve your growth and higher interests. Even worry has its role and purpose in the design. Emotions such as worry and anxiety are shown to activate additional (physical and cognitive) resources for goals that we find

important. Moderately optimal anxiety or worry has shown to enable rock climbers to climb better,[16] golfers to improve their putting performance,[17] and students to improve cognitive tasks.[18]

24. While worry, anxiety, and fear serve essential purposes in the design (fight or flight responses, heightened physiological states, etc.), they are often experienced unnecessarily in detrimental excess. In these cases they decrease effectiveness and strength of performance.[19] An especially fine line lies between beneficial anxiety and harmful anxiety. Navigating between the two is often cumbersome.

25. By recognizing the benevolent power of God-Creator's design, you activate additional cognitive and physical resources. These resources are set off without the experience of mental uneasiness that predisposes people to anxiety or fear. Recognizing the structure of God-Creator's design helps regulate emotions in accordance with the design's perfect coherence.

26. It is important to note that emotion regulation is not emotion avoidance. Attempting to avoid our emotions does not coincide with God-Creator's design. This merely exacerbates what we call undesirable emotions and can even cause depression.[20] Denying emotions, which are such a primary and personalized aspect of the design, can only disconnect us from its power.

27. It is important to remember that all things serve a vital and coherent purpose in God-Creator's design. This includes emotions. Emotions serve as action signals or catalysts, prompting us to keep or change course at any given time. You want to regulate your emotions so they guide your growth and serve your interests. This requires that you recognize their role in the overall design and not ignore them.

28. Clearly, there is a difference between recognizing your emotions as catalysts (positive or negative), and over-engaging in them. Constant rumination of worrisome or unconstructive emotions results in mental ailments like anxiety and depression.[21]

29. According to Tzvi Freeman's book, *Bringing Heaven Down to Earth*, Rebbe Menachem M. Schneerson said it well:

"Depression is not a crime. But it plummets a person into an abyss deeper than any crime could reach. Depression is a ploy instigated by the self-destructive elements within all of us. Once depressed, a person could do anything. Fight depression as a blood-sworn enemy. Run from it as you would run from death itself."[22]

30. Anger is also a most destructive emotion. Just as the Rebbe deemed depression a crime to the self, anger can result in a crime toward another. It is in your higher interests to avoid both.

31. Anger toward another person can escalate to thoughts and actions aimed toward revenge. When you recognize God-Creator's design and its lawful mechanisms, you know you needn't waste cognitive, emotional, and other resources on such action—regardless of how seemingly abundant these resources are. Your resources can always be more effectively utilized for your benefit or peace of mind (see also PART VIII on enemies).

32. Jesus Christ addressed avoiding counterproductive and, therefore, destructive anger when he shared the idea of loving your enemy as yourself. This does not mean to martyr yourself or have someone take advantage of you. It simply means to evaluate the actions of your enemy as you would your own. Any reactions based on this view will elicit far more powerful or enduringly influential results than those incited by vengeful anger. The only value in knowing the law is using it.

33. All unconstructive emotion-patterns cease when you recognize that all things occur by the divine design of an omni-loving, omnipotent God-Creator. This recognition aligns you with God-Creator's design and its power, thus ending the presence of any emotion-induced perspectives that do not serve you. New meanings are given to afflictive emotion states—meanings that foster growth toward godlikeness. When you retrain your mind according to this

perspective, your emotions regulate in perfect coherence with God-Creator's design. This can be done during meditation.

34. Meditation preceded by contemplation helps to regulate emotions. It reduces stress and unconstructive mood disturbances.[23] Even chronic emotional ailments benefit from perspective-changing meditation. Meditation is shown to cut depression relapses in half.[24] Indeed, routine meditation increases our basic happiness set-point.[25]

35. After just eight weeks of meditation, emotional contentment increases dramatically. This is, in part, because brain activity shifts from the right prefrontal cortex to the left prefrontal cortex.[26] A more active right prefrontal cortex induces feelings of discontent and anxiety. Conversely, when the left prefrontal cortex is more active, people feel fulfilled, strong, and purpose-driven.

36. With meditative practice the natural cycle of emotions is viewed for what it is: a tool for growth toward godlikeness, endowed by an omni-loving, omniscient God-Creator. As a side benefit, meditative practice increases the ability to sustain attention on important tasks. It also increases a person's tolerance for ultimately harmless things that were once considered stressful.[27] All of these internal mental benefits affect performance, behavior, and ultimately, success.

37. By retraining your mind to recognize God-Creator's design during meditation, you empower the physical structure of your brain. You align with God-Creator's powerful coherence at every level of your being—including your emotions and the actions they elicit. You rise to a higher level of godlikeness. This is reflected in your life as having the perfect home, the perfect car, the perfect career, and the most loving relationships...

38. Just as you would train your body for optimum health and power, you must train your mind as well. Retraining your mind for emotional coherence during meditation improves concentration, problem-solving skills,[28] and creative perception—even when you are not meditating. It enables you to focus on the aspects of God-Creator's design that contain opportunities for growth and development. This brings you closer to a godlike state of creational power. Your brain simply does not retrieve these opportunities and advantages during negative emotional states.

39. Many people attempt to ignore their emotions. They believe that emotions interfere with thought clarity. They think that rational thought processes are only hindered by emotion.

40. It is important, however, to remember that rational processes and emotional processes do not function in isolation. They are seen as distinct features of the brain

only for the purpose of human study. The truth is that these cognitive processes function in complete unison and neither one occurs without the influence of the other.

41. For this reason it is imperative that you acknowledge your emotions. By acknowledging them at any moment, you accurately discern whether you are in sync with God-Creator's design or acting in opposition to it. Where you are in opposition to it (or feel discontent, anxiety, depression, etc.), you can retrain your mind via contemplation, followed by meditation. This enables you to interpret events in a more favorable way, thus positively influencing your emotions. You gain supreme power.

42. This week, as much as possible, monitor your emotions. They often reveal the extent to which you are aligned with power or its opposite. If emotions are negative or unpleasant, it merely indicates that your perspective or interpretation of things is not serving you. In such cases, go into the silence. Retrain your mind according to the premises that all things occur in harmony with an omni-loving, omnipotent, omniscient God-Creator; that all things occur for your interest and benefit. Search for these benefits…you will find them. In this manner, negative emotions dissipate, and you align yourself with creative power, happiness, and love. Nothing is beyond doing (and everything is enjoyed in the process).

PART XIV

Inside Information On Islam, Christianity, and Israel

In accordance with evolutionary creation (the human journey toward godlikeness), all human conflict is a catalyst for growth. When we recognize that everything occurs by the design of an omni-loving God-Creator, the role of conflict as a catalyst becomes more evident. Accordingly, conflict becomes easier to manage, and its resolutions become more rewarding.

Global, interpersonal, and ideological conflicts incite development toward godlikeness. They are vital parts of evolutionary creation. Where we see conflict, humans are soon propelled forward; individual and collective power is gained.

Research shows that religious conflict, in particular, tends to be most intense.[1] The Israeli-Palestinian conflict over "God-given land" exemplifies this well.[2] It's important to remember that all religions and their opposing conflicts serve a divine purpose or they would not exist.

Even the persecutions that historically occurred in the name of religion served an essential purpose in the design. For humans to develop toward their current state of being, these and current conflicts were required.

We should therefore reconsider some of the key religious ideas that permeate our current paradigm so we can better understand both the past and present—which enables us to create a more fulfilling future for ourselves, our children, and others. It enables us to increase our wealth, improve our relationships, attain greater success, and experience more and more joy each day.

PART XIV

1. All that you have previously accepted as true (either consciously or not) influences the way that you process new stimuli. This is because humans process additional or new information by relating it to their mind and brain's existing information.

2. When new information does not properly fit in with a person's existing system of knowledge, the brain tends to classify the new information as false—the suggested ideas impossible. This is a psychological defense

mechanism. It is easier to process information that confirms that which we already believe as opposed to questioning the foundations that many of our thoughts rest upon (see more on the ego's mechanisms in PART II).

3. Such thought mechanisms can be useful, especially when considering mundane or unimportant issues. They allow for quicker processing by simply rejecting anything that cannot be processed with passive ease.

4. These psychological mechanisms are also useful when the information stored by the brain and mind coincides with the norms and ideas that are generally accepted by society and constructive. However, much of our existing thought foundations cannot be classified as such.

5. All too often the mind functions using outdated beliefs and assumptions that were better suited for previous social climates and their inherent situations.

6. This is due to the time lag required to absorb new scientific and other advanced knowledge en masse. However, when interpreting reality and new information in accordance with unconsciously held, outdated beliefs, the actions elicited are unconstructive at best. Earning the money you desire and cultivating the relationships you want becomes nearly impossible…

7. Outdated beliefs do not bring you closer to understanding the design and, therefore, do not serve your per-

sonal, social, or financial interests. Interestingly, many of the biblical interpretations that we rely upon for truth are outdated. These interpretations adversely influence the way we process new stimuli since they are part of the mind's existing body of knowledge. Much of our current human behavior explicitly reflects these outdated interpretive understandings.

8. In a universe designed by an omnipotent, omni-loving God-Creator, all things occur by design and must serve the designer's and designees' interest. No event can take place outside the fundamental design parameters established by this designer. This means that if something takes place, it must be constructive in that it coincides with God-Creator's benevolent design.

9. Thus, all biblical myths and biblical events serve a vital purpose in God-Creator's design, or they would not exist. The ways that we humans interpret these myths coincide with our level of godlikeness and with God-Creator's design. As evolutionary creation progresses, so does human godlikeness and people's biblical interpretations.

10. Judaism, Christianity, and Islam share ancestral roots, according to the Bible. These date back to Abraham. Abraham had two sons, each of a different wife, one son of a Jewish wife, the other of an Arab wife. The Arab son was first-born and named Ishmael. The Jewish son was second-born and named Isaac.

11. Ishmael had several children, including a daughter. Isaac had two sons (twins), Jacob and Esau. According to the stories presented in the Bible, Esau, as the first-born, was meant to be blessed by his father Isaac. However, Jacob is said to have tricked his blind father, Isaac, into receiving this blessing instead of Esau. A period of conflict between the twin brothers was created.

12. Esau eventually married Ishmael's Arabic daughter and founded a nation. Jacob founded the nation of Israel. These two nations were prophesied to engage in conflict by God-Creator's will and design—just as the brothers did. Part of the on-going conflict between Israelis and Arabs is said to indirectly stem back to this biblical story of the disputing twins. Of course there are countless, mundane, human explanations regarding the causes and effects of this conflict. However, this conflict coincides with God-Creator's omni-loving grand design, as do all conflicts.

13. In a world designed by an omnipotent God-Creator, no event can take place without being in alignment with God-Creator's (omni-loving) design. To indicate otherwise would be to detract from the meaning and concept of God-Creator as omnipotent. An omni-loving God-Creator considers the entirety of creation to be one. This God-Creator does not distinguish between nations or people. All events occur for the benefit of all involved.

14. When events incite conflict at a given stage of evolutionary creation, they act as catalysts for growth and development. They foster individual and community growth toward godlikeness (higher order, higher complexity, and greater harmony). As people strive to solve these conflicts, creative power is gained. If a conflict is addressed in a way that does not coincide with the laws of the design, this is soon learned via pain. As such, knowledge of the design is gained via experience. The processes involved in conflict resolution foster growth toward godlikeness.

15. All conflict is a result of human thought. The human mind has an innate tendency to misinterpret true cause and effect. When we see a small effect, we look for a prior event that was equally small. The mind then connects the two and deems the first event the cause and the second event the effect. The mind also does this with events it considers large.[3] These causal relationships are mentally (and collectively) formed, despite the fact that the events in question are almost never causally related. Indeed, there is no relationship between event size or magnitude when considering causal explanations.

16. This innate fallacy of human thought led many people to misinterpret the cause of the Jewish Holocaust. In accordance with this inherently misleading thought mechanism, many Christians asserted that the Jews suffered the Holocaust because they were responsible for crucifying Jesus Christ.

17. Most people considered the two events similar in size and magnitude. Accordingly, one must have caused the other, with the prior event (the crucifixion) as the cause for the one that followed later (the Holocaust); thus, the previously endorsed idea that Jews suffered the Holocaust for having killed Christ.

18. Historical accounts have shed light on the fact that both ancient Romans and Jews collectively collaborated to crucify Jesus Christ. At that time, Christ's preaching and following was considered a threat to Roman political order and a threat to Jerusalem's religious authority. Given the early stage of evolutionary creation at that time, the events played out as they did.

19. It is important to remember that nothing can occur outside the design of an omnipotent God-Creator. It is also important to recall that God-Creator is pragmatically omni-loving. All occurs under divine guidance by God-Creator's omni-loving design for the benefit of all creation.

20. Jesus Christ continues to serve a divine purpose in our evolutionary creation. For over 1.5 billion people, Jesus is the incarnation of God and, therefore, for them, is God or the Son of God in human form.

21. When considering his crucifixion, we must take into account that it is not possible for a human to kill God. The crucifixion of Jesus Christ occurred by divine

design. The event contained a divine purpose that is beneficial for human growth toward godlikeness, during the process of evolutionary creation. The crucifixion could not have happened otherwise.

22. These events were designed so that Jesus would be recognized as he is today (and has been for centuries). For this to happen, everything unfolded exactly as it did—to resurrect him, he was first crucified. For God-Creator's design to reach completion, this event had to occur (in myth or reality). The story and the human persecution it has caused should be recognized as vital to the completion of an omni-loving God-Creator's creation.

23. Whether Jesus Christ was God incarnate or a godlike prophet, healer, or preacher, his account serves a divine purpose in God-Creator's design. Its influence in Europe, the Middle East, both Americas and, really, all around the world has been enormous. In accordance with God-Creator's design, every person that believes that Jesus was God should believe this and those who do not, should not.

24. In a world designed by an omnipotent, omni-loving, omniscient God-Creator, all things serve a divine purpose. All things reflect humanity's current state of godlikeness. All things serve as catalysts for growth. This includes the existence of various religions and their followers, including their agreements, disagreements, wars,

persecutions, and eventual efforts to reconcile the differences between and among each other.

25. Pope John Paul II seems to have understood, more than many other papal leaders, the divine design and deeper meaning of the historically pervading dissonance between Jews and Christians. He accordingly established diplomatic relations with Israel[4] and apologized to Jews for the prior centuries of persecution. Indeed, part of the intense historical disagreement between Christians and Jews is due to the fact that their views are ultimately more similar than different. These disagreements have helped to cultivate greater godlikeness, growth, and development for all involved.

26. Despite their similarities, and an improved understanding between these two religions, official diplomatic relations between the Vatican and Israel are a fairly recent occurrence. This conflict, like any other, exists by the design of an omnipotent, omni-loving God-Creator. All conflict, at any point in evolutionary creation, is simply a catalyst for growth toward individual and collective godlikeness.

27. The historical conflict between Christians and Jews dates back to as early as the first century. History shows that both Jews and Christians have persecuted each other at various times and to varying degrees. This was typically done because of their different religious and political views.

28. After the crucifixion of Jesus Christ, Christians were persecuted by Romans—throughout the Roman Empire—and by Jews in what was formerly Palestine. It was not until Constantine the Great passed the Edict of Milan that Christianity became legal for practice in Rome. With the Edict of Milan, Jews could no longer live in Jerusalem.[5]

29. Soon the Council of Nicea convened under Constantine. Here, Catholic bishops reached consensus on basic matters of the Christian faith. This meeting institutionalized the Roman-Christian Empire and furthered the persecution of Jews. Such events helped to fuel a long Jewish Diaspora.

30. The intricate mechanisms of God-Creator's design are such that you cannot affect one thing without influencing all others. Recognition of this truth fosters cohesive thought and cohesive action in all things. It is the fount of creative power. The design should be seen and analyzed as it is: cohesive and lawful, not scattered or inconsistent. As you understand and resemble (in thought and action) the design's coherence, so you exhibit even higher degrees of its power.

31. As anything else, the Jewish Diaspora is part of God-Creator's design. It caused Jews, unlike any other nation, to be dispersed throughout the world. Prior to their semi-collective return to Israel after World War II, their homes

were in European, American, and other world cities. Both the Jews and their hosting nations benefited from these cultural immersions in many ways, including philosophically, genetically, scientifically, and financially to name a few. Monotheism—the belief in one God—flourished.

32. Although Christians and Jews have some differences in their views and interpretations of some events, they both identify with the idea that there is only one God (monotheism). Monotheism has become the basis for legal, philosophical, and cultural systems in Europe and the Americas.

33. Indeed, monotheism forms the deepest foundation of all Western civilization. Western democracy is simply a governing construct of a monotheistic people. As Western-style democracy spreads, so do the seeds of monotheism upon which it stands and Abraham's philosophical descendants (monotheists) are multiplied *beyond number, like the stars in the sky and the sand on the seashore*[6]—a feature of evolutionary creation prophesied in the Bible.

34. It is clear that the Jewish Diaspora impelled greater unification among previously ideologically separated monotheistic religions. During the Diaspora Christians and Jews lived and developed side by side. This enabled Jews to fully immerse themselves in and contribute to the growth of some of the world's most prosperous nations, prior to the many returning to Israel. The mutual

benefits were and continue to be enormous. This sharing of cultures and environment enabled both groups to collectively grow toward greater godlikeness.

35. It is known that culture and environment affect all aspects of a person's thinking. In fact, environmental and cultural influences alter the structure and functioning of our brains[7] and genomes. As a result of the Diaspora, Jews (as those who "delivered" monotheism) and their hosting nations underwent genetic and psychological advancement at the most basic cellular levels.

36. As concerns biological science, epigenetics shows that environmental and cultural factors influence the structure of our genes. It works as follows: epigenomes are on top of your genes and switch your genes on and off in response to environmental factors and the way they are interpreted. This process of de-activating genes is called DNA methylation[8] whereas the process of activating genes is called histone modification.[9]

37. The genetic changes that result from environmental factors are transferred to our offspring. Having fully acclimated to countries and cities all over the world, the genetics of Jews and their hosting nations were—to a certain extent—transformed as a result of the Diaspora.

38. Upon returning to Israel after World War II, Jews were a changed nation. Their genes were differently

programmed and activated. Their psychological make-ups and brain physiology had changed relative to their Middle Eastern cousins and brothers. They had been influenced by Western knowledge and cultural development. After years of worldwide persecution, they returned to Israel to face a unique challenge.

39. Just as Biblically prophesied, the Israeli nation found itself in conflict with the now largely Muslim Arabs. In this conflict the Israelis had—and continue to have—the upper hand in the situation. As one of the strongest armies in the world,[10] Israel defends itself against a far less sophisticated but still numerically overwhelming and dangerous Arab-Muslim nation. The Israelis' military sophistication, ability, and desire to defend their nation are reflections of many factors, including, but not limited to, the pre-designed Diaspora.

40. As with all humans, everything that the Jewish people experienced during the Diaspora is biologically and psychologically encoded in their bodies.[11] The more influential the experiences, the more engrained is the corresponding code. Any biological changes that result from experience are transferred to future generations of that person's offspring.

41. The Jews who have returned to Israel have centuries of varying degrees of persecution engrained in their DNA. It is thus painful and nearly impossible for them to harmfully persecute another group of people. Despite

their great military organization and motivation, they try to defend themselves as humanely as possible against a much more populated surrounding Arab-Islamic world.

42. Indeed, Israel is the native land of Jews. They originated there in the Middle East. In accordance with biblical history, they share genetic lineages with Arabs like that of brothers. Having spent centuries genetically (physically, intellectually, and emotionally) co-mingling with Christians, the Jews in Israel are now the potential bridge between the Arab-Islamic and Judeo-Christian worlds.

43. The Israeli-Arab conflict is not solely contained to the Middle East. Israel is currently designed to be the heart of a much more global ideological experience—one between Judeo-Christians and the radical segments of Arab-Muslim countries. In fact, Israel is the only established Western-style democracy in the Middle East to date.

44. The manner by which the Judeo-Christian and Muslim cultures ultimately resolve this global conflict will demonstrate (and increase) their level of godlikeness.

45. The key to resolving this and all conflicts is to understand God-Creator's design, as much as possible; to recognize that all things occur by the design of an omni-loving, omnipotent God-Creator. In this manner your interpretations of all things change; they are viewed in the most beneficially constructive ways.

46. Conflicts are simply catalysts for growth and development toward godlikeness. They help fuel evolutionary creation. Without them it is suggested that people would not progress. Jesus Christ, one of the greatest prophets, also known as the son of God, likely understood this and declared, "Perhaps people think that I have come to cast peace upon the world. They do not know that I have come to cast conflicts upon the earth: fire, sword, and war."

47. While conflict is a necessary catalyst for growth, the highest growth is achieved in conflict resolution. A master key to resolving conflict rests in the statement: "Love your enemy as yourself." This does not mean to martyr yourself. Part of growth toward godlikeness entails respectful self-preservation. The Torah states, "If one comes to slay you, slay him first."[12] However, as humans progress toward godlikeness, their Biblical interpretations of such statements must also evolve.

48. We must remember that the Bible is multi-dimensional and written in metaphor. To "slay" another more likely implies that one must protect and guard himself to ensure growth and endurance—as killing is entirely condemned in the Ten Commandments.

49. It is clear that conflict resolution requires creativity. And creativity occurs only when we are in alignment with God-Creator's design. The design is the fount of all

power…to act against it is to reduce your access to this power.

50. For your exercise this week, recognize the value and purpose of conflict both in your own (personal and business) life and on a more global scale. Begin resolving any potential conflicts in your life. Conflicts can be draining and inevitably affect seemingly unrelated aspects of a person's life (on personal and global scales). Beneficial conflict resolution requires creative genius, which means you should enter the silence prior to resolving conflict. When individual and global conflicts are resolved, higher states of godlikeness are achieved. Growth, advancement, and their inherent powers are gained.

51. Where we see conflict we see a lack of comprehension or recognition of God-Creator's design. We see a need for growth toward godlikeness, since true godlikeness surpasses the need for conflict. As you resolve your conflicts creatively and beneficially, higher godlikeness is obtained, the implications of which are gigantically in your favor.

"I tell you that if two of you on earth are in agreement about anything you ask for it will be done for you by my Father in heaven. For, where two or three come together in my name there am I with them."[13]

—Jesus Christ

PART XV

What We Need to Know to Create Our Lives the Way We Want Them to Be

Determinism, pre-determinism, and free will have been apparently incompatible for centuries. Different schools of theologians and philosophers have vigorously debated the issue without reaching any real unified conclusion.

However, as humanity intellectually and scientifically progresses, people unveil additional components of God-Creator's design. This allows everyone to better understand how apparently separate aspects of the design cohesively function together in one whole. In this way the relationships between previously irreconcilable ideas become more apparent. Creativity flourishes…which means that you enjoy more harmonious relationships, you gain the ability to have the career you've always wanted, and you earn the money you desire…

For instance, science continues to reveal that the laws upon which the universe functions are deterministic. These deterministic laws direct the process of evolutionary creation (the collective journey toward human godlikeness). This is what is meant by the term "deterministic evolutionary creation."

The human concept and feeling of having day-to-day free will is also a pre-determined part of God-Creator's design. As a person becomes more godlike, he or she acquires greater free will. Humans are still developing completely godlike free will. It is important to remember that the act of creation (the human journey toward godlikeness), is still in progress.

Becoming more godlike requires attaining higher levels of spiritual and practical knowledge. For this to occur, the laws upon which the design functions must be better understood. We can then utilize their mechanisms for our personal and collective human benefits. Part XV discusses these mechanisms—and the findings from which they are derived.

PART XV

I. Determinism refers to the idea that all events and conditions are caused by previous events and conditions. Thus, all things, including thought and behavior, are determined by prior (recent) states.

2. Pre-determinism asserts that all events and conditions are caused by previous events and conditions dating all the way back to the universe's origins. No current forces can alter this preset sequence of events and conditions. According to this view, people have no influence in creating their future.

3. The idea of free will asserts that humans *do* have the ability to influence their realities. With active free will, conditions are decided by human thought and behavior and conditions are not pre-determined; rather, we create them ourselves.

4. The ideas of determinism, pre-determinism, and free will have seemingly been incompatible for centuries. Theologians, philosophers, and now scientists have been struggling with this apparently contradictory question. In accordance with evolutionary creation (the collective human journey toward godlikeness; the act of creation), intellectual, scientific, and technological progress all shed new light on this issue.

5. Science continues to unveil the law-driven mechanisms that determine the universe's functions. While universal laws influence all outcomes of existence, humans have yet to uncover all of these laws and the intricacies with which they function.

6. The laws that have been discovered and are included in *A Guide to Your Supreme Power* can be used for your

advancement—your growth and development toward godlikeness. Toward higher sophistication, power, complexity and individual and social harmony.

7. Each law reveals an additional aspect of God-Creator's design and the mechanisms through which it functions. With each new discovery, humans gain greater power. We gain the insight required to utilize these mechanisms for our development (technological, business, personal relations, etc.).

8. We humans are an integral part of the design, including our brains, bodies, and, as many believe, our souls or spirits. Some neuroscientists assert that our brains determine our thoughts and therefore our behaviors. This view essentially asserts that people are biological "human robots" whose actions contain no free will.[1] Accordingly, your thoughts and their resultant actions are little more than the totality of your genes, nerve cells, and their molecules interacting lawfully and determinately.[2] As potentially convincing as the argument is, it obviously uncovers only a small part of the design.

9. Free will is another key aspect of God-Creator's design. The fact that free will has been such an enduring topic of study indicates that God-Creator has embedded the concept of free will in human intellect. We should remember that this intellect (as a function of the human brain and nervous system) was also created by God-Creator.

10. The ongoing discussion of free will (and any other similarly reoccurring subject) is a necessary component of our experience in evolutionary creation. It is a catalyst, in that it causes us to search for answers—for knowledge. It drives human progress and development. Many times our scientific developments serve as "human proof" for already long-standing religious ideas.

11. The truths or laws for which science seeks are often indirectly and indistinctly preserved and promoted in the myths of the Qu'ran, the New and Old Testaments, and essentially all divine / spiritual writings. In accordance with God-Creator's design, humans further uncover these truths via the Tree of Knowledge (the Tree of Knowledge is a metaphor for science and experience—both of which uncover key aspects of the design). Indeed, the Tree of Knowledge bears the fruits of science and human experience. Both religion and science, by the same design, are catalysts for growth and development on our journey toward godlikeness.

12. As for science, although the brain and related physical laws are said to determine our life outcomes (according to current knowledge), the brain's cellular structure is entirely influenced by our experiences[3] and more importantly, our interpretations of them. Since we can influence and control our interpretations, then, relative to our human needs free will is unlimited. *A Guide to Your Supreme Power* gives you greater power over your interpretations, thus increasing your free will.

13. When you contemplate and meditate in accordance with the view in *A Guide to Your Supreme Power*, you increase your growth and development. It enables you to change the chemical and cellular structure of your brain[4] for your advantage. Your brain then influences your thoughts, which manipulates genome activation and, ultimately, influences the known physical laws that are said to determine the results you secure. Despite this complexity some people theorize that the outcome of these mechanisms can be fully predicted.

14. To accurately predict a person's behavior, we would need to know the initial state of the trillions of molecules in his or her body. Solving such an equation with our current state of knowledge would take billions of years.[5] This estimate does not consider the fact that the mind directly influences the structure of the brain. This potentially alters the equation's components exponentially. Current science cannot yet determine the outcome of three particles interacting with each other let alone this more complex, multi-faceted equation.[6]

15. Science is designed to be deterministic; however, much of the universe's functions remain unknown; science is not yet complete. Our human ability to determine things is thus equally incomplete. The more we discover God-Creator's design, the more we realize that there is no discrepancy between divine determinism and human free will. As we grow more godlike, we learn that the world is not as deterministic as many once tended to believe.

16. The word "determinism" may need to be redefined or replaced with a different meaning to serve our future intellectual needs. Albert Einstein said, "God does not play dice." Niels Bohr responded by saying, "You cannot tell God what to do." It is likely that both of them were correct when discussing the physical universe.

17. While deterministic Newtonian laws accurately predict certain phenomena in this world, these laws do not describe the whole of creation. The theory of relativity and the science of quantum mechanics made clear the limitations of Newtonian physics. We still lack most of the information regarding the universe's mechanisms.

18. Humans continue to uncover aspects of the design bit by bit. For example, neuroscientist Benjamin Libet found that between a brain signal and our conscious response to it is a 100-millisecond period during which free will may exist.[7] According to Libet, it is during these 100 milliseconds (of a 500–1,000 millisecond-response process) that we unconsciously decide to act or not to act on a particular signal emitted by the brain. Technically speaking, whether free will or other still-unknown forces occupy those 100 milliseconds will be better understood in the future.

19. Given the limits of human intellect and knowledge when compared to God-Creator, there is no real human authority as concerns the subject of divinity. However, as humans progress in evolutionary creation,

more knowledge is uncovered. In accordance with God-Creator's omni-love, information is given exactly when it will be most beneficial for the whole of creation (so the participants in its creation will not accidentally destroy themselves).

20. For example, Maimonides, a great medieval Torah scholar, once affirmed that the world was deterministic. He stated that if God-Creator is omniscient, then the impending actions of each human are already known. Indeed, a person's actions were already determined, meaning that there was no free will.[8] Given the available human knowledge during Maimonides's lifetime, this ancient view was likely appropriate. However, in light of humanity's current intellectual and scientific state, this perspective is now outdated.

21. As we progress in evolutionary creation, we become more godlike. We gain more knowledge of the laws that guide the design. This increases our personal power—which includes free will. However, our degree of free will is contingent upon acting in accordance with God-Creator's design. For example, we are limited in that we cannot tamper with or destroy the design. Such knowledge would be provided only when all people are godlike—when it would not be used intentionally or accidentally by anyone for destructive purposes. This includes destruction of other people, the earth, or other parts of the universe.

22. Once we reach total godlikeness, we humans will be full co-creators of our world. Indeed, your degree of free will and creative influence coincides with your degree of godlikeness. *A Guide to Your Supreme Power* directs you toward higher degrees of free will, power, sophistication, complexity, and harmony. Your ability to secure the things you desire (the cars, the homes, the career, the family, the partners, etc.) increases.

23. It is God-Creator's interest that the act of evolutionary creation reaches completion. This is why individual development or godlike advancement precedes new levels of knowledge. As we evolve to be more powerful, creative…godlike, we begin to see the relationships between things that initially appeared diametrically opposed.

24. Incompatibilism upholds the idea that free will and determinism are logically opposed. Many Christians once translated God-Creator's omnipotence, omniscience, and omnipresence to mean that humans have no free will. Today, with progress in evolutionary creation, this is changing. As we become more godlike, creativity develops, and we see the connections between seemingly disconnected ideas. This is essential for success and advancement in all things.

25. Still, sometimes discovering the fixed mechanisms with which the universe functions causes humans to reactively assume that there is no free will. For instance, upon discovering that time is not a linear function—but rather

a dimension like that of space—physicists asserted that the past and future must be concretely determined.⁹ But as depositories of truth, religious traditions preserve knowledge that ultimately prevents us from accepting such conclusive ideas at their outset. There is a reason for this, as all aspects of God-Creator's design are purpose-driven.

26. For example, Jewish traditions support the notion of free will. Many Jews claim that the part of the soul that is united with God-Creator (called *yechida*) is the part of a person that has free will. This closely aligns with the fact that the more a person is godlike, the greater degree of free will that person has.

27. Where a person understands and functions in accordance with the laws of God-Creator's design, that person's free will is relatively unlimited—especially when considering our human desires in relation to the universe's workings as a whole. We cannot create the universe yet but we can create our lives the way we want them to be!

28. The Zohar (Kabbalah scripture) similarly indicates that we are partners in God-Creator's act of creation. According to Kabbalah, our actions are not only free but they also affect aspects of reality that are completely unknown to us.[10]

29. We are limited in action only by the laws of God-Creator's design; however, as we progress toward godlikeness,

apparent limitations become perceivable advantages. As we gain knowledge of the design's mechanisms, we increase our levels of free will and power. This means that we can secure more happiness and wealth in all areas of life.

30. Science reveals that the laws of God-Creator's design are fixed and guide the courses of events. Understanding how the design functions is advantageous. It enables us to work in sync with the parameters of the design, as opposed to against them. We come to realize that all things are in a way determined—but the meaning of "determined" is relative. Things are determined only in that they are lawfully driven. However, when we understand the laws and mechanisms of the universe, free will (our ability to influence these mechanisms) is gained.

31. To endorse complete determinism, as it is defined today, is to assume that we have reached a state of absolute knowledge, where all of God-Creator's laws are known to us. Under such assumptions, no person can be said to act freely. A person's thoughts and behavior are predefined, based on past circumstances and the manner by which his or her brain recorded them—both of which were equally predefined.

32. In God-Creator's design, nothing functions in isolation. In accordance with the Zohar, all things affect all others. The complete acceptance of determinism is no exception.

33. According to a deterministic view, no one can be held responsible for his or her actions.[11] Punishment in accordance with current criminal law could not be justified. If the brain single-handedly determines the mind, and the brain is driven by predetermined, physical mechanisms, the criminal cannot be held responsible.[12] Indeed, the entire justice system would need to be restructured to accommodate this understanding. It is worth noting that those who are benevolent and kind would be equally undeserving of praise.

34. Some neuroscientists who vouch for determinism believe that all thought and behavior arises from the brain. As your brain is structured, so you act. For example, the part of the brain called the prefrontal cortex plays a key role in social behavior.[13] It is known that repeat violent offenders or people with anti-social personality disorder (APD) have a differently structured prefrontal cortex.

35. Research shows that people diagnosed with APD have thinner volumes of gray matter in their prefrontal cortex...and less neural activity. The prefrontal cortex is less developed and less active. It is therefore structured differently from the prefrontal cortex of those without APD.[14]

36. Similarly, the anterior cingulate is the part of the brain that controls inhibition. This part of the brain is

less active in people who exhibit impulsive aggression. When exposed to chemicals that usually incite inhibition, an unusually aggressive or violent person's brain does not respond as expected.[15] In fact, research continues to unveil that much behavioral tendency is rooted in the structure and functioning of the brain.

37. If our actions are generated as a result of our physical brain structures, are we personally responsible for our actions? Are criminals responsible for their crimes?

38. Since the brain can be physically modified by will, each person is ultimately accountable for his or her actions—good or bad. So the answer to the above questions is yes. Everyone can implement more favorable actions, according to the principles outlined in *A Guide to Your Supreme Power*. When you train your mind in accordance with God-Creator's design, you also change your brain. You are rewiring your brain to serve you. Thought patterns become more constructive, and actions become more beneficial. You align yourself with power thereby gaining a degree of power and freedom yourself.

39. Even people who have been diagnosed with APD can increase the volume of matter in their prefrontal cortex. Doing so would diminish the severity of their behavior, as people who meditate are shown to have more gray matter in this part of the brain. When you retrain your brain in accordance with God-Creator's design,

impulsivity is lessened and brain waves become more coherent. Brain waves also become more powerful and faster.[16]

40. God-Creator's design functions according to universal laws and fixed mechanisms. Although these unchanging (from a human viewpoint) mechanisms determine the parameters by which we function, we have relatively unlimited free will. This means that even in a seemingly deterministic world, people can act freely. The more godlike a person is, the more free will that person has. Free will requires knowing the parameters of the design and acting in sync with them. In this manner, a person influences universal mechanisms in the most creative, constructive ways.

41. Events are determined by all—known and as yet unknown—physical laws of nature. According to frontier science, the physical laws of your brain and body determine your thoughts and behavior—and ultimately the conditions of your life. When you recognize God-Creator's design and retrain your mind accordingly via contemplation and meditation, you increase your level of free will. You begin retraining your brain, DNA, and body in a way that serves your interests. You become the creator of your reality.

42. This week, before going into the silence, contemplate the recognition that a person's godlikeness determines his or her level of free will. A person cannot truly

influence a thing until he or she knows how it functions, how it is designed, how it works. To be godlike is to have knowledge of God-Creator's design. It is also to embody the qualities of an omni-loving, omniscient God-Creator as much as possible. In this manner humans progress forward, more pleasantly, more rapidly. Life is more rewarding and fulfilling.

43. Once all humans discover and internalize the laws that drive God-Creator's design, the act of evolutionary creation will be complete. At that point, a state of complete godlikeness and the global agreement it fosters is attained. This is the heaven of which the Old Testament, Jesus Christ (and others) often spoke.

44. By retraining your mind during meditation, in accordance with the spiritual and psycho-biochemical-physical laws outlined in *A Guide to Your Supreme Power*, you become more godlike. This means that your levels of power, happiness, fulfillment, wisdom, and joy increase. The decisions you make each day reflect your progressive growth and advancement. Enormous creative power is gained, the advantages of which are gigantic.

45. When a person retrains his or her mind in accordance with the laws mentioned in *A Guide to Your Supreme Power*, he or she begins to naturally react to key events and circumstances in the most beneficially constructive ways. The result is complete and total success in all

things (health, finance, relationships, etc.) and a much more enjoyable, loving, joyous experience of life.

46. As you become more godlike, you are able to create your circumstances with ease and stress-free joy. Your interpretations of reality serve you. You begin securing the full support and power of God-Creator's design, as opposed to acting against it. This is to become more godlike, the current perfection of which is your final, on-going exercise.

MEDITATION

The Key to Retraining Your Mind for Happiness, Success, and Joy

1. The most effective way to retrain and empower your mind, using principles of neuroscience, is via meditation. When you retrain your mind during meditation, creativity and personal power develop. You also cultivate the many other advantages mentioned in this chapter such as being able to have, be, or do anything that you want.

2. With meditation you can rewire your brain in accordance with key, core ideas that better serve you. The strengths and benefits of doing so are far more than science can yet determine. However, we will mention some of the truths unveiled by frontier science so far.

3. We will also mention some of the more intangible, experiential benefits of meditating that will likely be

understood by science in the future. As humans grow more godlike they will gain the knowledge required to uncover the currently intangible (or spiritual) mechanisms that underlie meditation.

4. Contemplation followed by meditation is perhaps the only presently known way by which humans can access omniscience. The act of meditation allows us to do this by quieting the mind and ultimately transcending it. As we quiet our mind's "chatter," we allow space for new "omni-based" knowledge to enter. This is the way to contact the best consultant and receive ultimate professional guidance in all things. When practiced with *A Guide to Your Supreme Power*, meditation is your ultimate shortcut to success.

5. While this process of accessing higher knowledge and divine guidance is not yet fully understood by science, this does not mean it does not exist. Science is still trying to unveil most of the intricate mechanisms of this universe.

6. As John Polkinghorne (a well-known physicist and theologian) mentioned, "Reality is very rich, many-layered. Science, in a sense, explores only one layer of the world."[1] The contributions of science are necessary (by design), but we should keep in mind that they are inevitably limited by our current human knowledge and the instruments we have created to examine reality thus far.

7. Perhaps more scientifically verifiable is the fact that meditation enables people to transcend egocentric thinking. An overactive ego prevents us from acquiring information that does not simply confirm the things we already believe. As a result people often mentally cut themselves off from knowledge and information that is pertinent to the enduring success of their endeavors and causes.

8. With meditation, we can retrain our minds to our advantage. Of course, to realize a most empowering, cohesive thought structure, it is important to contemplate prior to meditating; contemplation and meditation are two different but complementary mental activities.

9. Prior to entering the silence via meditation, you should contemplate on the knowledge enclosed in *A Guide to Your Supreme Power*. This enables you to recognize that all things occur by the design of an omni-loving God-Creator for your benefit. This means that nothing can occur outside of this all-loving, all-knowing power. All things serve a divine, beneficial function for your growth and development toward godlikeness or they would not exist.

10. The benefits of a situation may not always be readily apparent to the human mind; but when we have trained our minds to know they are there, we look for them. And when you search for the benefits in all things, you inevitably find them.

11. *A Guide to Your Supreme Power* has outlined many of the known advantages that this specific perspective brings. The creative power gained from retraining your mind and brain to recognize these ideas is unimaginable. The results are more success, happiness, fulfillment, health, and less worry, concern, needless fear, anxiety, etc. The effects are life-changing for the better—you need only experience them for yourself to truly comprehend them. Meditation is a primary tool for these and even better results.

12. When you are familiar with the practice of contemplation and meditation, you can and should contemplate anything you think is important prior to entering the silence. Thus, you (and your affairs) are guided by powerful omni-knowledge that obviously exceeds our collective human knowledge to date. Your actions coincide with God-Creator's designed system.

13. Some people prefer to affirm a specific prayer prior to entering the silence of meditation. Each person should do what he or she feels is most beneficial for his or her circumstances, preferences, and goals. Once you have grown accustomed to seeing the underlying, benevolent design in all things, you are naturally guided to do that which is best for your needs and desires.

14. Despite the fact that the scientific study of meditation is fairly new, frontier science has already unveiled some of the benefits to be gained by meditating.

15. For example, most people's sympathetic nervous systems have evolved to hyper-respond to the slightest external pressures. When this occurs, cortisol, adrenaline, and all stress-response hormones flood the brain and body.[2] Thought, emotion, and immunity are adversely affected. Creative power is suspended until the homeostatic imbalance is overcome.

16. For this reason, it is helpful to strengthen the *parasympathetic* nervous system, the system that regulates restful states. The *sympathetic* nervous system predominates under stress and elicits the fight-or-flight response.

17. When you meditate you strengthen your parasympathetic system to slightly dominate the sympathetic nervous system. By lessening sympathetic nervous system activation,[3] hyper-responses to stress are eliminated. The body becomes retrained for stabilized strength rather than stress-induced over-responsiveness.

18. Stress-induced responses to mundane occurrences can increase heart rate and cause high blood pressure, both of which are undesirable for strong cardiovascular health. Meditation is shown to balance both heart rate and blood pressure.[4] Indeed, meditation is shown to be more effective at reducing blood pressure and heart rate than typical biofeedback and rest.[5]

19. Unnecessary stress responses affect the entire body and brain. Once the hormones cortisol and norepinephrine flood a person's system, creativity is suspended, pseudo-panic sets in, and immunity decreases. However, the mere act of meditation is shown to decrease the production of stress-induced cortisol while increasing immunoreactivity.[6,7]

20. Since meditation reduces the presence of the stress-induced hormone cortisol, it has neuroprotective effects on the brain and body.[8] This decreases and even reverses aging. Research shows that after just a few months, those who meditate have the biological structure of a person who is five to twelve and twenty years younger than his or her calendar age.[9]

21. In addition to preserving mental and physical vibrancy, meditation may strengthen neural circuits, which increases cognitive capacity, the results of which are higher intelligence, faster reaction time, and greater creativity.[10]

22. In fact, after just a few days of approximately thirty or so minutes of meditating, a person's attentional ability increases.[11] By further activating the brain's executive attention networks, meditation can increase higher-order cognitive processing and help reduce the number of task errors that a person makes.[12] Consequently, a person's day-to-day functioning becomes superior. Performance

skyrockets, personal relationships improve, you make more money, and you gain the ability to change anything.

23. Advantages of meditating extend beyond cultivating higher attention and increasing performance; meditation also improves mood. It helps to reduce fatigue and anxiety, both of which strongly influence our mental functioning. Anxiety reduction, in particular, enables people to be more open to the ideas of others, thus increasing creative opportunities and abilities.

24. The act of closing oneself off to the ideas of others is often due to an overactive ego. With regular meditation, we not only transcend an overactive ego, but the brain becomes better synchronized and its knowledge better integrated.[13] Increased brainwave synchronization fully propels creative genius. These changes can also improve a person's ability to monitor conflicts and sustain cognitive control.[14]

25. Increased cognitive control reduces the tendency to ruminate or have repetitive (unconstructive) thoughts. The tendency to think unconstructive thoughts over and over leads to depression.[15] By interfering with or weakening this mental pattern, meditation reduces depression.[16] Depression can likely be eliminated in full when a person retrains his or her mind and brain in accordance with the perspective included in *A Guide to Your Supreme Power*.

26. In fact, meditation reduces many forms of psychological distress, such as anger, worry, and other adverse emotional tendencies.[17] By releasing the neurotransmitter GABA into the brain and body, meditative practice relieves potential anxiety or tension.[18] These changes improve emotional well-being on the most basic biochemical level.

27. Increased emotion regulation often translates into better health and functioning, overall. Imbalanced emotional states can be uncomforting and disruptive. This sometimes prompts people to engage in ultimately damaging, addictive behaviors, like smoking, drinking, or drug use.

28. By interrupting negative thought patterns, meditation helps to overcome damaging addictions.[19] This is because meditation enables us to transcend our mental activity. When we become aware of our thoughts as thoughts and nothing more, we can observe or witness our thought patterns without necessarily acting upon them. This is to have greater godlikeness or free will.

29. A person's mind may produce any number of thoughts that are related to an addictive habit. However, when we don't act on that thought, the neural networks that trigger that particular addiction are weakened. When we consciously choose not to act on that thought trigger enough times, the neural networks upholding the

addiction dissipate, and the (potentially physical) addiction is overcome...*A Guide to Your Supreme Power* can help you eliminate these addictions painlessly.

30. Indeed, meditation re-stabilizes and restructures a person's entire being for his or her benefit. Creative power and strength are inevitably gained. While many strengthening physical qualities have been discovered in relation to meditation, other less quantifiable strengths can be gained by meditative practice. These improvements are often deemed metaphysical since humans have not yet pinpointed the mechanisms by which they function.

31. For example, it is said that, when people meditate, they transcend mundane thought boundaries that inhibit creativity.[20] Transcending these boundaries enables people to be more playful, positive, and liberated. Joy accompanies such heightened awareness and transcendent understanding—joy that cannot be understood by the intellect alone.

32. With meditation, people witness more so-called "divinity" in previously underappreciated things. Mundane stress is replaced with a new cognitive flexibility and joy. There is greater inner peace than ever before; a person's psychological experiences and actions soon reflect this. Life as a whole improves. While the benefits of meditation are many, these benefits are greatest when you recognize the perspectives outlined in *A Guide to Your Supreme*

Power ... including the idea that the world is coherently designed by an omni-loving, omnipotent God-Creator.

33. The best way to experience and cultivate the strength and joy that meditative silence offers is to enter the silence yourself. Many options are available for learning how to meditate; TM meditation centers and Mindfulness meditation centers are seemingly everywhere—these and other techniques work well with the ideas outlined in *A Guide to Your Supreme Power*.

34. You can also use the fifteen to thirty-minute meditation instructions included below.

- ❖ Sit down in a quiet place where you will not be interrupted.
- ❖ Contemplate.
- ❖ Close your eyes and take deep breaths to help yourself relax.
- ❖ Clear yourself of any potentially negative influences.
- ❖ Gradually enter into deeper dimensions of awareness within yourself.
- ❖ Ask for transcendent wisdom related to your goals and desires.
- ❖ Stay quiet and peacefully still in transcendent awareness.

❖ Give gratitude and emerge from the silence, gradually…(affirm that you will feel refreshed and invigorated upon exiting—no dizziness, confusion, or nausea).

Once you have become accustomed to entering the silence, you will appreciate it more and more. Upon retraining your mind and brain to recognize God-Creator's cohesive design, you gain enormous creative power. Doubt and stress are replaced with constructive happiness.

"Where there is peace and meditation there is neither anxiety nor doubt."

—St. Francis of Assisi

References

Part I
1. Hawking, S., and Mlodinow, L. 2010. *The grand design.* New York: Bantam Books.
2. Theories of the universe: Scientific origins of the universe—Infoplease.com http://www.infoplease.com/cig/theories-universe/scientific-origins-universe.html#ixzz1H8dsPdnE.
3. Hawking, S., and Mlodinow, L. 2010. *The grand design.* New York: Bantam Books.
4. Russell, Peter. 2001. *iGenetics.* New York: Benjamin Cummings.

Part II
1. Hilton, Denis J. 2001. The psychology of financial decision-making: Applications to trading, dealing, and investment analysis. *The Journal of Psychology and Financial Markets* 2.1:37–53.
2. *Ibid.*
3. Matlin, Margaret W. 2009. *Cognitive psychology.* Hoboken: John Wiley & Sons.
4. Truluck, Janet E., and Bradly C. Courtenay. 2002. Ego development and the influence of gender, age, and educational levels among older adults. *Educational Gerontology*:325–336.

5. *Ibid.*
6. Nisbett, Richard E., and Timothy DeCamp Wilson. 1977. Telling more than we can know: Verbal reports on mental processes. *Psychological Review* 84.1:231–259.
7. Lapinski, Maria Knight, and Franklin J. Boster. 2001. Modeling the ego-defensive function of attitudes. *Communication Monographs* 68.3:314–324.
8. Gendolla, Guido H. E., Kerstin Brinkmann, and Dorothea Scheder. 2008. Ego involvement moderates the assimilation effect of affective expectations. *Motivation and Emotion*:213-220.
9. *Ibid.*
10. http://www.counselingcenter.illinois.edu/?page_id=191.
11. Gendolla, Guido H. E. and Michael Richter. 2005. Ego involvement and effort: Cardiovascular, electrodermal, and performance effects. *Psychophysiology*:595–603.
12. *Ibid.*
13. *Ibid.*
14. http://socialanxietydisorder.about.com/od/relateddisorders/a/anxietyillness.htm.
15. Campbell, Keith W., et al. 2003. Responding to major threats to self-esteem: A preliminary narrative study of ego-shock. *Journal of Social and Clinical Psychology* 22.1:79–96.

16. Lapinski, Maria Knight and Franklin J. Boster. 2001. Modeling the ego-defensive function of attitudes. *Communication Monographs* 68.3:314–324.
17. Campbell, Keith W., et al. 2003. Responding to major threats to self-esteem: A preliminary narrative study of ego-shock. *Journal of Social and Clinical Psychology* 22.1:79–96.
18. *Ibid.*

Part III

1. Arntz, William, Betsy Chasse and Mark Vicente. 2005. *What the bleep do we know!?* Deerfield Beach: Health Communications, Inc.
2. *Ibid.*
3. Begley, Sharon. 2009. *The plastic mind.* London: Constable & Robinson Ltd.
4. *Ibid.*
5. Arntz, William, Betsy Chasse, and Mark Vicente. 2005. *What the bleep do we know!?* Deerfield Beach: Health Communications, Inc.
6. Luders, Eileen, et al. 2009. The underlying anatomical correlates of long-term meditation: Larger hippocampal and frontal volumes of gray matter. *NeuroImage* 45.3:672–678.

Part IV

1. Baldauf, Sarah. 2010. Our genes, not the whole story. *U.S. News & World Report*:24–26.

2. Arntz, William, Betsy Chasse and Mark Vicente. 2005. *What the bleep do we know!?* Deerfield Beach: Health Communications, Inc.
3. Hamilton, Dr. David R. 2008. *It's the thought that counts.* Carlsbad: Hay House Inc.
4. *Ibid.*
5. *Ibid.*
6. Chopra, Deepak. 1989. *Quantum healing: Exploring the frontiers of mind/body medicine.* New York: Bantam Books.
7. Arntz, William, Betsy Chasse, and Mark Vicente. 2005. *What the bleep do we know!?* Deerfield Beach: Health Communications, Inc.
8. *Ibid.*
9. *Ibid.*

Part V

1. Lucey, Brian M. and Michael Dowling. 2005. The role of feelings in investor decision-making. *Journal of Economic Surveys* 19.2:211–237.
2. Taleb, Nassim Nicholas. 2007. *The black swan.* New York: Random House.
3. *Ibid.*
4. Grosse, Robert. 2010. The global financial crisis—a behavioral view. Working paper. Monterrey: EGADE Graduate Business School.
5. *Ibid.*
6. *Ibid.*

7. Fischhoff, B., P. Slovic, and S. Lichtenstein. 1977. Knowing with certainty: The appropriateness of extreme confidence. *Journal of Experimental Psychology: Human Perception and Performance* 3:552–564.
8. *Ibid.*

Part VI

1. Matt. 18:19–20 (New International Version).
2. *Ibid.*
3. Mooney, Linda A., David Knox, and Caroline Schacht. 1994. *Understanding social problems.* Dixon: Google Books.
4. Thagard, Paul. The moral psychology of conflicts of interest: Insights from affective neuroscience. *Journal of Applied Philosophy* 24.4:367–380.
5. *Ibid.*
6. Naqvi, Nasir, Baba Shiv, and Antoine Bechara. 2006. The role of emotion in decision making: A cognitive neuroscience perspective. *Current Directions in Psychological Science* 15.5:260–264.
7. Peterson, Richard L. 2007. Affect and financial decision-making: How neuroscience can inform market participants. *The Journal of Behavioral Finance* 8.2:70–78.
8. Sanfey, Alan G., and Luke J. Chang. 2008. Multiple systems in decision making. *Annals of the New York Academy of Sciences* 1128.1:53–62.

9. Horan, Roy. 2009. The neuropsychological connection between creativity and meditation. *Creativity Research Journal* 21:199–222.

Part VII

1. Parks, Colleen M., and Jeffrey P. Toth. 2006. Fluency, familiarity, aging, and the illusion of truth. *Aging, Neuropsychology, and Cognition*:225–253.
2. Arntz, William, Betsy Chasse, and Mark Vicente. 2005. *What the bleep do we know!?* Deerfield Beach: Health Communications, Inc..
3. Callender, Craig. 2010. Is time an illusion? *Scientific American*:58–65.
4. Drosnin, Michael. 1997. *The Bible code.* New York: Simon & Schuster.
5. *Ibid.*
6. Justo L. Gonzalez. 1970–1975. *A history of Christian thought*: Volume 2. *From Augustine to the eve of the Reformation.* Abingdon Press.

Part VIII

1. Gordon, Carol, and Asher Arian. 2001. Threat and decision-making. *Journal of Conflict Resolution*:196–215.
2. *Ibid.*
3. Kandel, Eric R. 2006. *In search of memory: The emergence of a new science of mind.* New York: W.W. Norton & Company, Inc.

4. Eldar, Sharon, et al. 2010. Enhanced neural reactivity and selective attention to threat in anxiety. *Biological Psychology* 85.2:525–257.
5. Arntz, William, Betsy Chasse, and Mark Vicente. 2005. *What the bleep do we know!?* Deerfield Beach: Health Communications, Inc.
6. Ehrman, Bart. 2004. *Truth and fiction in the Da Vinci Code: A historian reveals what we really know about Jesus, Mary Magdalene, and Constantine.* New York: Oxford University Press.
7. Lindberg, Carter. 2006. *A brief history of Christianity.* Blackwell Publishing.
8. Robinson, James M. 1990. *The Nag Hammadi Library.* New York: Harper Collins.
9. Meyer, Marvin, and James M. Robinson. 2007. *The Nag Hammadi Scriptures: The revised and updated translation of sacred gnostic texts complete in one volume.* New York: HarperCollins.
10. Robinson, James M. 1990. *The Nag Hammadi Library.* New York: Harper Collins.
11. *Ibid.*
12. Matt.18:19–20 (New International Version).

Part IX

1. Merali, Zeeya. 2011. Physics of the divine. *Discover*:49–52.
2. Cooper, David A. 1997. *God is a verb: Kabbalah and the practice of mystical Judaism.* New York: Riverhead Books.

3. Laurenceau, Jean-Philippe, Lisa Feldman Barrett, and Michael J. Rovine. 2006. The interpersonal process model of intimacy in marriage. *Journal of Family Psychology* 19.2:314–323.
4. *Ibid.*
5. *Ibid.*
6. Robbins, Anthony. 1991. *Awaken the giant within.* New York: Simon & Schuster Inc.
7. Laurenceau, Jean-Philippe, Lisa Feldman Barrett, and Michael J. Rovine. 2006. The interpersonal process model of intimacy in barriage. *Journal of Family Psychology* 19.2:314–323.
8. Da Vidas, Eliyahu. Soulmates. http://www.chabad.org/kabbalah/article_cdo/aid/380433/jewish/Soul-Mates.htm.
9. http://www.sciencedaily.com/videos/2008/0403-men_are_from_mars.htm
10. Laurenceau, Jean-Philippe, Lisa Feldman Barrett, and Michael J. Rovine. 2006. The interpersonal process model of intimacy in marriage. *Journal of Family Psychology* 19.2:314–323.
11. Koball, Heather L., et al. 2010. What do we know about the link between marriage and health? *Journal of Family Issues* 31.8:1019–1040.
12. Lee H.J., A. H. Macbeth, J. H. Pagani, and W. S. Young. 2009. Oxytocin: The great facilitator of life. *Progress in Neurobiology* 88.2:127–51.

13. http://www.kabbalah.info/engkab/life-love-family/kabbalah-relationships.
14. Clark, Margaret S., et al. 2010. Ways of giving benefits in marriage: Norm use, relationship satisfaction, and attachment related variablity. *Psychological Science* 21.7:944–951.
15. *Ibid.*
16. Shusterman, Yosef. 1998. Parshat tetzaveh. *Beverly Hills Chabad Newsletter* 1.17.
17. Freeman, Tzvi. 1997. *Bringing heaven down to earth.* Class One Press.
18. http://www.eurofound.europa.eu/areas/qualityoflife/eurlife/index.php?template=3&radioindic=54&idDomain=5 & http://www.cdc.gov/nchs/fastats/divorce.htm.

Part X

1. Thomson, Helen. 2010. Alpha, beta, gamma: The language of brainwaves. *New Scientist.*
2. Arntz, William, Betsy Chasse, and Mark Vicente. 2005. *What the bleep do we know!?* Deerfield Beach: Health Communications, Inc.
3. Byrne, Rhonda. 2006. *The Secret.* New York: Atria Books.
4. Robinson, James McConkey, and Richard Smith. 1988. *The Nag Hammadi Library in English.* The Netherlands: Brill.

5. http://www.hawking.org.uk/index.php/lectures/64
6. Born, Max. 1926. *The Born-Einstein Letters,* trans. Irene Born Walker and Company, New York, 1971.

Part XI

1. Rajiv, Saini. 2010. Antioxidants accelerates cellular health. *International Journal of Green Pharmacy*:212.
2. http://www.antiaging-systems.com/ARTICLE-613/theories-of-aging.htm
3. Becker, A. J., et al. 2002. Growth hormone, somatomedins and men's health. *The Aging Male* 5.4:258–262.
4. Robbins, Anthony. 1986. *Unlimited power.* New York: Free Press.
5. Perricone, Nicholas, M.D. 2004. *The clear skin prescription.* New York: Harper-Collins Publishers Inc.
6. *Ibid.*
7. Huddleston, Dan E., et al. 2007. An in vivo correlate of exercise-induced neurogenesis in the adult dentate gyrus. *Proceedings of the National Academy of Sciences of the United States of America*:5638–5643.
8. http://www.nomeatathlete.com/stu-mittleman/.
9. http://www.peertrainer.com/how_to_train_your_body_to_burn_fat_and_have_more_energy.aspx.

10. Chopra, Deepak. 1989. *Quantum healing: Exploring the frontiers of mind/body medicine.* New York: Bantam Books.
11. Begley, Sharon. 2009. *The plastic mind.* London: Constable & Robinson Ltd.

Part XII

1. Thomas J. Glover, comp. 2003. *Pocket Ref*, 3rd ed. Littleton: Sequoia, which in turn cites Geigy Scientific Tables, Ciba-Geigy Limited, Basel, Switzerland, 1984.
2. Carroll, James. 2001. *Constantine's sword: The Church and Jews.* New York: Houghton Mifflin.
3. http://learningtogive.org/papers/paper222.html.
4. http://www.jewishworldreview.com/0111/prager.php3.
5. http://nlt.scripturetext.com/genesis/22.htm.

Part XIII

1. Lucey, Brian M., and Michael Dowling. 2005. The role of feelings in investor decision-making. *Journal of Economic Surveys* 19.2:211–237.
2. Ibid.
3. Ibid.
4. http://www.kabbalah.info/.
5. Myers, D. G. 2004. Theories of emotion. *Psychology*: 7th ed. New York, NY: Worth Publishers.

6. http://www.affective-sciences.org/system/files/2005_Scherer_SSI.pdf.
7. Myers, D. G. 2004. Theories of emotion. *Psychology*: 7th ed. New York, NY: Worth Publishers.
8. Thagard, Paul. 2007. The moral psychology of conflicts of interest: Insights from affective neuroscience. *Journal of Applied Philosophy* 24.4:367–380.
9. *Ibid.*
10. Robbins, Anthony. 1991. *Awaken the giant within.* New York: Simon & Schuster Inc..
11. Baum, Andrew, Neil E. Grunberg, and Jerome E. Singer. 1992. Biochemical measurements in the study of emotion. *Psychological Science* 3.1:56–60.
12. *Ibid.*
13. Palacios R., and I. Sugawara. 1982. Hydrocortisone abrogates proliferation of T-cells in autologous mixed lymphocyte reaction by rendering the interleukin-2 producer T-cells unresponsive to interleukin-1 and unable to synthesize the T-cell growth factor. *Scandinavian Journal of Immunology* 15.1:25–31.
14. http://www.integrativepsychiatry.net/neurotransmitter.html.
15. http://www.integrativepsychiatry.net/neurotransmitter.html.
16. Beal, Daniel J., et al. 2005. An episodic process model of affective influences on performance. *Journal of Applied Psychology* 90.6:1054–1068.

17. Siddique, Hoorie I., et al. 2006. Worry, optimism, and expectations as predictors of anxiety and performance in the first year of law school. *Cognitive Therapy and Research*: 667–676.
18. Chamberlain, Sean T., and Bruce D. Hale. 2007. Competitive state anxiety and self-confidence: Intensity and direction as relative predictors of performance on a golf putting task. *Anxiety, Stress, and Coping.* 20.2:197–207.
19. Beal, Daniel J., et al. 2005. An episodic process model of affective influences on performance. *Journal of Applied Psychology* 90.6:1054–1068.
20. Kumar, Sameet, Greg Feldman, and Adele Hayes. 2008. Changes in mindfulness and emotion regulation in an exposure-based cognitive therapy for depression. *Cognitive Therapy and Research*:734–744.
21. *Ibid.*
22. Freeman, Tzvi. 1997. *Bringing heaven down to earth.* Class One Press.
23. Kumar, Sameet, Greg Feldman, and Adele Hayes. 2008. Changes in mindfulness and emotion regulation in an exposure-based cognitive therapy for depression. *Cognitive Therapy and Research*:734–744.
24. Begley, Sharon. 2007. What the Beatles gave science. *Newsweek.*

25. Begley, Sharon. 2009. *The plastic mind.* London: Constable & Robinson Ltd.
26. *Ibid.*
27. Kumar, Sameet, Greg Feldman, and Adele Hayes. 2008. Changes in mindfulness and emotion regulation in an exposure-based cognitive therapy for depression. *Cognitive Therapy and Research*:734–744.
28. Begley, Sharon. 2009. *The plastic mind.* London: Constable & Robinson Ltd.

Part XIV

1. Pearce, Susanna. 2005. Religious rage: A quantitative analysis of the intensity of religious conflicts. *Terrorism and Political Violence* 17.3:333–352.
2. Plante, Thomas. 2009. A commentary on religious conflicts and a call for a focus on the best the traditions have to offer. *Pastoral Psychology* 58.1:73–78.
3. Nisbett, Richard E., and Timothy DeCamp Wilson. 1977. Telling more than we can know: Verbal reports on mental processes. *Psychological Review* 84.1:231–259.
4. http://www.jewishvirtuallibrary.org/jsource/anti-semitism/jp.html.
5. http://www.religioustolerance.org/jud_pers1.htm.
6. http://nlt.scripturetext.com/genesis/22.htm.

7. http://psychcentral.com/news/2010/08/04/cultural-environment-influences-brain-function/16380.html.
8. http://www.time.com/time/health/article/0,8599,1951968-2,00.html#ixzz1B38mjB6L.
9. Baldauf, Sarah. 2010. Our genes, not the whole story. *U.S. News & World Report*:24–26.
10. http://www.globalfirepower.com/.
11. Hamilton, Dr. David R. 2008. *It's the thought that counts.* Carlsbad: Hay House Inc.
12. http://www.science.co.il/Arab-Israeli-conflict-2.asp.
13. Matt. 18:19–20 (New International Version).

Part XV

1. Hawking, Stephen, and Leonardo Mlodinow. 2010. *The grand design.* New York: Bantam Books.
2. Crick, Francis. 1994. *Astonishing hypothesis: The scientific search for the soul.* New York: Touchstone.
3. Hamer, Dean H. 2000. A three-billion-year memoir. *Scientific American*:114–116.
4. Begley, Sharon. 2009. *The plastic mind.* London: Constable & Robinson Ltd.
5. Hawking, Stephen, and Leonardo Mlodinow. 2010. *The grand design.* New York: Bantam Books.
6. *Ibid.*

7. Gazzaniga, Michael S., and Megan S. Steven. 2005. Neuroscience and the LAW. *Scientific American Mind*.
8. Gorfinkle, Joseph, ed., antn., trans. 1966. *The eight chapters of Maimonides on ethics (Semonah Perakhim)*. New York: AMS Press.
9. Editorial. 2002. The chronic complaint. *Scientific American*:10.
10. *Zohar I:35a*
11. Farah, Martha J. 2009. *Neuroethics*. New York: Springer Publishing Co.
12. Gazzaniga, Michael S., and Megan S.Steven. Neuroscience and the LAW. *Scientific American Mind*.
13. *Ibid.*
14. *Ibid.*
15. *Ibid.*
16. Dobbs, David. 2005. Zen gamma. *Scientific American Mind*:9.

Meditation

1. Tippett, Krista. 2010. *Einstein's god*. New York: Penguin Books.
2. Lemonick, Michael D., and David Bjerklie. 2003. A frazzled mind, a weakened body. *Time* 161.3.
3. Curiati, Jose Antonio, et al. 2005. Meditation reduces sympathetic activation and improves the

quality of life in elderly patients with optimally treated heart failure: A prospective randomized study. *The Journal of Alternative and Complementary Medicine* 11.3:456–472.

4. Solberg, Erik E., et al. 2004. Hemodynamic changes during long meditation. *Applied Psychophysiology and Biofeedback* 29.3:213–221.

5. Ibid.

6. Tang, Yi-Yuan, et al. 2007. Short-term meditation training improves attention and self-regulation. *PNAS* 104.43.

7. Greeson, Jeffrey M. 2008. Mindfulness research. *Complementary Health Practice Review* 14.1:10–18.

8. Xionga, Glen L., and P. Murali Doraiswamy. 2009. Does meditation enhance cognition and brain plasticity? *Longevity, Regeneration, and Optimal Health*:63–69.

9. Chopra, Deepak. 1989. *Quantum healing: Exploring the frontiers of mind/body medicine.* New York: Bantam Books.

10. Xionga, Glen L., and P. Murali Doraiswamy. 2009. Does meditation enhance cognition and brain plasticity? *Longevity, Regeneration, and Optimal Health*:63–69.

11. Zeidan, Fadel, et. al. 2010. Mindfulness meditation improves cognition: Evidence of brief mental training. *Consciousness and Cognition*:597–605.

12. van den Hurk, Paul A. M., et. al. 2010. Greater efficiency in attentional processing related to mindfulness meditation. *The Quarterly Journal of Experimental Psychology*:1168–1180.
13. Horan, Roy. 2009. The Neuropsychological Connection Between Creativity and Meditation. *Creativity Research Journal*:199–222.
14. Zeidan, Fadel, et. al. 2010. Mindfulness meditation improves cognition: Evidence of brief mental training. *Consciousness and Cognition*:597–605.
15. Schreiner, Istvan, and James P. Malcolm. 2008. The benefits of mindfulness meditation: changes in emotional states of depression, anxiety, and stress. *Behaviour Change*:156–168.
16. *Ibid.*
17. Greeson, Jeffrey M. 2009. Mindfulness research update: 2008. *Complementary Health Practice Review* 14.1:10–18.
18. Dakwar, Elias, and Frances R. Levin. 2009. The emerging role of meditation in addressing psychiatric illness, with a focus on substance use disorders. *Harv Rev Psychiatry*:254–267.
19. Greeson, Jeffrey M. 2009. Mindfulness research update: 2008. *Complementary Health Practice Review* 14.1:10–18.
20. Horan, Roy. 2009. The neuropsychological connection between creativity and meditation. *Creativity Research Journal*:199–222.

www.ingramcontent.com/pod-product-compliance
Lightning Source LLC
Chambersburg PA
CBHW050554170426
43201CB00011B/1687